PAUL

BY

WILLIAM WREDE

TRANSLATED BY

EDWARD LUMMIS

WITH PREFACE BY

J. ESTLIN CARPENTER

Wipf and Stock Publishers

EUGENE, OREGON

Wipf and Stock Publishers
199 West 8th Avenue, Suite 3
Eugene, Oregon 97401

Paul
By Wrede, William
ISBN: 1-57910-567-X
Publication date: January, 2001
Previously published by American Unitarian Association, 1908.

Published in Boston by the American
Unitarian Association in 1908

PREFACE

THE Apostle Paul is presented to us in the pages
of the New Testament in various aspects. He is
the agent of the great expansion of Christianity,
who carried it from Syria to Asia Minor, from
Asia Minor to Greece, and converted it from a
sect of the Jews into a religion for the world. He
is the champion of liberty, who set the new faith
free from the yoke of the Law. He is the preacher
of life in the Spirit, showing men the 'upward
way' to the noblest ethical heights, and cheering
them with immortal music in the Psalm of Love.
Not only is he the intrepid missionary, he is the
organizer of Churches, knit together by an exalted
theory of organic unity in Christ. And besides
this, he is a thinker of extraordinary boldness,
compelled by the necessities of his work to justify
the Gospel, on the one hand to his own country-
men, and on the other to the Gentiles. He does
so by reasonings which are often difficult to follow ;

partly because his presuppositions are different from ours; partly because the letters which he has left are not complete or systematic expositions of his teaching; and partly because his thought is rooted in a profound personal experience which has rarely been repeated, and is consequently difficult fully to apprehend.

In one respect, indeed, the student of the Apostle's thought has an advantage denied to the student of the Gospels. We have the actual words which Paul wrote, while only a very few of those which Jesus spoke have been transmitted to us in his native tongue. True, not all the letters bearing Paul's name may have been written at his own dictation; true, we do not know for certain the year in which he was converted, the dates of his correspondence with the Churches, the time and place of his death. But these things are not necessary for the understanding of his ideas. What is essential for that purpose is that the interpreter should come to his words through the modes of thought and feeling belonging to Paul's own time, rather than through the fabrics of doctrine which theologians of a later day have reared upon them.

Such a guide is to be found in the late Prof. Wrede, of Breslau, whose lamented death in November, 1906, removed from the field of New Testament study a brilliant investigator and a teacher of profound sincerity and earnestness. Into the sketch which these pages contain he has condensed the results of laborious years. He is not afraid to describe the Apostle as a man rather than as a saint ; and he does not find his significance for Christian history impaired because he can no longer accept the forms in which the preacher of the crucified Messiah presented the person of Jesus and the meaning of his death. But he shows us how these forms arose in Paul's mind out of the circumstances of his own history, the school of thought in which he had been brought up, and the work to which he felt himself called. Doubtless other interpretations are possible of some of Paul's great doctrines. The careful reader will readily find many questions which this little book does not answer. In its brief limits important aspects of the Apostle's teaching are inevitably ignored. But the writer puts into the hand of the inquirer a clue which will help him to make his way through many obscure and

difficult places. The central conceptions of the
Pauline scheme are disengaged with singular
clearness ; and the theological construction which
made the Apostle to the Gentiles 'the second
founder of Christianity ' is estimated in its relation
to the needs of the age as well as the personality
of the teacher. / Those who plead that the Church
should go 'back to Jesus,' must never forget
that but for Paul there would (humanly speaking)
have been no Church at all.)

J. ESTLIN CARPENTER.

OXFORD, 7 *July*, 1907.

AUTHOR'S PREFACE

THE aim of the following pages is not to give a biography of Paul, but to characterize his personality, ministry, religion, and historical significance. Completeness, in view of the abundance of the material, could not be attempted. It must suffice to bring out what is essential. The reader will find supplementary matter in several directions in other numbers of this series of ' Popular Books on the History of Religion,'[1] especially that by Vischer on the Letters of Paul, that by von Dobschütz on the Apostolic Age, and that by Jülicher on Jesus and Paul.

A popular exposition of the Pauline theology is beset with especial difficulties. To give a real idea of it, such as the general reader can grasp, without going into its detail, is unfortunately beyond the resources of art. I could not make up my mind to

[1] Religionsgeschichtlichen Volksbücher, edited by Lic.-theol. Friedrich Michael Schiele, of Marburg; published by J. C. B. Mohr, Tübingen.

dispose of it summarily, because it is in this theology, to a very great extent, that the historical importance of Paul is to be found ; but I have tried to describe it as concisely and clearly as I could. Those who do not care to read the whole chapter are directed to the sections ' The Chief Lines of Paul's Christology,' ' The Doctrine of Redemption,' and ' The Origin of the Doctrine.'

The evidence for the view I take of Pauline doctrine, which may strike many readers as strange, cannot of course be set out in any great fulness in the narrow limits of such a work as this. Those readers, however, who wish to go into these questions more thoroughly will find references (in foot-notes) to at least a *selection* of authenticating passages, with some few elucidations ; so also with the remaining sections. . . . . A certain amount of literature on Paul is noted in an appendix.

Those who desire to read the letters of Paul together with this work should certainly make use of a modern translation. . . . .

W. WREDE.

BRESLAU, 5 *December*, 1904.

CONTENTS

INTRODUCTION

SOURCES

In the age when Christianity was coming into being, Paul is the clearest, even in a certain sense the only clear figure. After his death there follows a long period in which *not one* Christian, not to speak of an important one, stands palpably before us. How shadowy seem to our eyes the immediate disciples of Jesus, even such a one as Peter! And even Jesus himself is for us much more difficult of access than his greatest apostle. We can only see his form as through a rolling mist. Much is entirely covered; some part is clouded over less thickly; yet another part, indeed, is clear to view—the mist has parted.

Our testimonies to Jesus are only later accounts, which were not put together by eyewitnesses. The amount of true information which they unquestionably contain is overlaid with thick layers of legendary adornments and historical

fancies, prompted by the faith of the later communities; it is only after a weary labour of
discrimination, beset on all sides by many uncertainties, that we can hope to come near to
the core. But for Paul we possess in a true sense
original authorities, as authentic as any document
can be which is a product of the history for which
it vouches. In his letters we catch to-day the
tones of his own voice, unmuffled and free from
any distracting sound, without any other toil
than that of interpretation.

But even these sources certainly give us very
far from all that we might wish. It is only here
and there that they throw a ray of light, often
no very clear one, on the life and fortunes of
the man. But they do give us just that which,
in a hero of religious history, is most important—
they show us much, very much, of his mental
shape, and this not doubtfully mirrored in another
soul, but true to life, as it was, in its innermost
and deepest self. They carry us in the most
vivid way into the missionary labour which made
up his daily work. They set before our eyes the
religious thinking of the apostle, in fragments
indeed and sections, but still in its many-sided-

ness and with the stamp of character ; in fine they show us, without intending it, the image of Paul the man and the Christian.

Thirteen letters have come down to us under the name of Paul. The following account is based upon the view that eight of these really emanate from Paul, namely, the first letter to the Thessalonians, that to the Galatians, the two to the Corinthians, the letter to the Romans, that to the Colossians with the short note to Philemon, and that to the Philippians. Very serious considerations make against the Pauline origin of the second Thessalonian letter, still more serious against that of the letter to the Ephesians, and the most serious of all against that of the so-called Pastoral Epistles (to Timothy and Titus). We, together with a great number of critics, on grounds into which we cannot enter here, hold these five letters to be spurious.[1] On the other hand, the letter to the Colossians, which has often been associated with these, may with good reason be defended as a genuine writing. Whether one letter more or less is genuine or

[1] Vischer, in his ' Letters of Paul,' takes a more favourable view of II Thessalonians and Ephesians.

spurious is after all of small account. It is only
the genuineness of the Pastoral Epistles that
would *essentially* affect the figure of Paul.

The view disseminated in Holland, and heard
also here and there in Germany, that all the
Pauline letters belong to a later time, can
only be regarded by us as a critical aberration.
Such letters as I Thessalonians, Galatians, II
Corinthians, point in a hundred indications and
allusions as definitely as possible to conditions
which are only conceivable within a few decades
of the death of Jesus. And the forger is yet to
be born who could devise such unforced, individual,
purely personal utterances, born of the moment,
as are here found in abundance, and at the
same time make the letters as a whole seem to
reveal in their author a fixed, finished, original
personality.

All the genuine letters fall into the last period
of Paul's life. Hardly a decade separates the
earliest from the latest. It is to be regretted
that the intervals are not longer, and that we have
not at command any such testimonies from his
own hand dating from the spring-time of his
Christianity. How differently might we then be

able to measure the development of Paul! The material we possess tells us little enough of the incipient Christian and thinker.

Otherwise it is of a fairly various kind. We have highly personal letters by the side of highly impersonal, letters to communities known and un-known to the writer. Here the questions of the life of the community preponderate, there learned dissertation or polemic, there again the treatment of special events and individual relations.

These letters find a supplement—except for a few isolated traditions, the only one—in the Acts of the Apostles. But, to the eyes of the author of that book, the clear physiognomy of Paul has already faded. It has given place to the general apostolical countenance, such as Peter also exhibits in the same book. Paul's speeches have, after the fashion of ancient his-torians, been conferred by the author on his hero; they are not reports of real discourses; and the historical presentment affords some highly astonishing features, both in detail and in sum. Nevertheless its value is considerable. The author possessed, especially for the history of Paul, excellent original matter, and has worked

more or less of it into his book.   In some passages,[1]
at least, we hear the voice of a real personal
acquaintance and travel-companion of Paul. Without this book we should in any case have had no
clue to the course of the Pauline mission, at
least to its later stages. It gives us also much
precious detail concerning the labour and the
experiences of the apostle, and it even shows us
some sides of his work with which the letters do
not sufficiently acquaint us.

[1] In chapters 16, 20, 21, 27, 28, where the word ' we '
appears in the narrative (the ' we-passages ').

I

THE MAN

1—His Youth. His Conversion

PAUL[1] was descended, as he himself states with emphasis upon occasion, from a genuine Jewish family. The social layer to which he belonged, if not a high one, must still be thought of as not among the lowest. His home was Tarsus, the capital of Cilicia, even if his actual birth must be assigned, according to a tradition which comes to light in the fourth century in Jerome, to the small Jewish town of Gishala ; otherwise he would not be spoken of in the Acts of the Apostles as ' of Tarsus.'

Tarsus was a great city, highly Hellenistic,

---

[1] Alongside this Greek (or properly Latin) name he used the Jewish name of Saul. Double names such as this, more or less similar in sound, were not unusual.

and not merely a provincial capital, but also an important centre of culture, and in particular a seat of the Stoic philosophy. But we must not infer from this that Paul himself necessarily fell under the influence of Greek culture to any special extent. In the Jewish quarter of all great cities there were houses enough whose orthodox atmosphere denied admittance to the Hellenism which breathed around them. If Paul attached himself to that Jewish sect whose observance was most strict, the Pharisees, and if he was intended for a Rabbi, this points to a parental house which was only slightly affected by the relaxing spirit of general culture, by which so many Jews of the Dispersion had been smitten.

Nevertheless, it was by no means an insignificant fact that he grew up amid Greek surroundings. He gained so much from them that he was able to become, in later days, ' to the Greeks a Greek.' Above all he mastered, in early youth, the Greek language, and learned to read the Greek Bible. But a language is never a merely formal thing ; imperceptibly it carries and imparts ideas. It was then no slight matter for him to be brought into close observation of Greek ways and modes

of thought. Even if he would have none of them
at the time, they might nevertheless acquire
importance at a later period. And besides,
even the more strict and faithful Judaism among
the Dispersion had long since adopted certain
Greek conceptions and views, which were no
longer felt to be Greek. Some of these appear
in the letters of Paul,[1] and are tokens of this
indirect Greek influence; their actual extent is
variously estimated. Finally we find traces,
which point in the same direction, of some degree
of schooling. It is true that Paul never betrays
an acquaintance with real philosophic thought,
and in making use, as he once does, of a quotation
from a poet,[2] he is only doing what many do
who know nothing of literature and possess no
library. But his style is nevertheless remarkable.
Amid all its laboured movement and palpable
inaccuracy there may often be perceived a sense
of rhetorical form, and especially of rhythm in
the articulation and rounding of his sentences,

[1] Cf. e.g., the concept *conscience* (I Cor. 8[7] sqq. and other
places) and (in part) the use of the word *flesh*.

[2] The passage in I Cor. 15[33], ' Evil communications corrupt
good manners,' comes from the Comic Poet Menander.

such as he could hardly have acquired without
stylistic instruction and practice. Let the reader
recall only, as one instance, the construction of
that supremely beautiful hymn on love.[1]

Still, in the main, the culture of Paul is the
culture of the Rabbis. He had sought it at
its source. He went to Jerusalem. The Acts
of the Apostles makes him a disciple of the
celebrated Rabbi Gamaliel.[2] This assertion has
been doubted, but perhaps wrongly. Whether
it be true or false, the certainty that Paul did
go through the Rabbinical school is established
by his own letters. The signs they exhibit are
too plain to be mistaken. We must not be
misled by the fact that he had learned the craft
of a weaver of tent-cloth. Smiths, joiners,
shoemakers, and other handicraftsmen are to be
found among the Rabbis.

What was learned at Jerusalem might be the
whole width of the heavens apart from what
was understood as 'culture' in Rhodes, Corinth,
Rome, or even in Tarsus, but it was none the
less a kind of culture. Paul possessed a very

[1] I Cor. 13.   [2] Acts 22³.

keen intellect, which was developed in this school in a definite direction. The art of dissecting maxims, drawing conclusions from premises, following up whole chains of inference, rebutting objections—in brief, of exercising in religious questions what one may call a forensic method of dealing with evidence—all this he had learned in Jerusalem ; and with it, of course, the art of subtle polemic.

All these data relate merely to the outfit of the man. In his pre-Christian period we can find only one trait which throws light on his character, but that is indeed a Pauline characteristic ; it is his ' zeal,' the zeal which impels him to the utmost exactness in the observance of the Law, and makes him the violent persecutor of the followers of Jesus.[1] This young Jew has the countenance, no doubt, of the genuine fanatic. His soul is on fire. He is goaded by the ambition to excel his contemporaries in all that Judaism means,[2] and he knows how to hate with the hatred which none but the believer, hating the unbeliever, can attain. But his fanaticism is not of the base

---

[1] Gal. 1^{13} sq. Phil. 3^5 sq. [2] Gal. 1^{14}.

kind. The later Paul makes that clear enough. Its root is his love for his religion. Warfare against false belief is for him a duty towards God.

* * * * * * * *

The career of the Pharisaic zealot came to a swift and sudden end. Paul belongs to that rare class of men whose lives, by a single event, are cut clean in two. A cleft strikes down into the depths of his being. He becomes another man, and lives thenceforward in the consciousness that he is another man, that he has received, so to speak, a new self, a new 'I.' There is something portentous in such an experience. It fills the whole inner life of the man with an inextinguishable sense of contrast between then and now. It sets up one great guiding star for all his thought and perception. It endows him with a concentrated determination such as the desultory mass of men find unattainable.

Paul hated Jesus. He looked upon him as a leader of religious sedition and a false Messiah, whose death as a criminal on the cross was the best evidence of what the man really was. But on the way to Damascus—for even there the orthodox champion sought to harry the scattered disciples—he beheld this Jesus in celestial light, and was overcome with the irresistible conviction, a judgment as it was upon his life up to that moment, 'The crucified lives : he is therefore indeed the Messiah.' This moment decided his life.

What happened ? Paul has not himself given us any account of the event, but only touched upon it allusively here and there.[1] In the Acts of the Apostles we find a description—indeed, three. There is a central kernel in all of them which agrees with Paul's own hints, but the obvious contradictions in the three accounts[2] are enough to arouse distrust of all that goes beyond this kernel.

So much is sure—Jesus cannot have stood in the body before his enemy. Paul's own views and conceptions are also decisive on this point. For Paul knows no resurrection of the flesh. He does indeed ascribe a body to those that have risen, but a 'spiritual,' immaterial body, such

[1] Gal. 1[15] sq. I Cor. 15[8] ; 9[1]. Cf. II Cor. 4[6]. Phil. 3[7] sqq.

[2] Acts 9, 22, and 26. 22[9], for instance, says of Paul's companions, ' They saw the light, but heard not the heavenly voice.' 9[7] says the contrary.

a body therefore as the outer senses cannot perceive. If then he believed that he had looked
upon the risen Jesus, this cannot have been any
'seeing' in the ordinary, 'carnal' sense, no
actual seeing with eyes. It was a vision, and
visions are events that take place within the
human soul, and are products of the human
soul, even though the visionary may have no
other thought but that his eye receives pictures,
his ear tones, from without.[1] So far as we can
tell, Paul never doubted that he had really seen
Jesus. If the doubt ever arose, it must have
been instantly overcome by faith. In its effect
upon him the vision had the full force of an
objective fact.

There lay, of course, adequate causes behind
this occurrence, just as much as behind those
visions of a living Savonarola, which some saw
after his death. Its roots must have lain in Paul's
nature, in impressions which he had received,
in convulsions of soul. But it is another matter
whether we are in a position to expound those
causes. He certainly knew of appearances of

[1] Some theologians speak of 'objective visions.' but that
is not a scientific conception.

Christ, in which the disciples of Jesus gloried, and it was not a matter of small moment that they occupied his thoughts, and set the pattern for his own experience in that kind. Such visions have indeed an inductive, even an infectious power. But if we seek to fathom more deeply what it was that then lived in his soul, suppositions are cheap, but knowledge is dear. Whether, for instance, the heart of the persecutor was especially moved by the courage with which the disciples confessed their faith, whether by words of Jesus, who is bold enough to say?

The event must always remain shrouded in uncertainties. But one thing is certain. Paul had not been previously won over by teaching, to which the vision was a mere appendage. He expressly denies that human instruction had any part in the foundation of his faith. For him the vision must have had the character of something sudden and overpowering. In the mid course of hatred, it may be, he was struck by the beam of divine light. But even then the vision did not come without preparation. For while fanatical hatred asserts itself on the surface, still in the depths, without the man perceiving

it, doubt may be gnawing, ferment and revolution
may be at work, and a new thing be fighting
its way upward.

The great change which the apparition wrought
in Paul did not lie in the moral region. As a
Pharisee he had served God with passionate
devotion and deep sincerity, and lived for his
will. He needed not, like other 'converts,'
converts from a life of sin, to turn away from
sensual pleasure and love of the world, that he
might be thenceforward a penitent and holy
man. The fault of his former life, as he sees it,
is not even his hardness and intolerance, but
simply and singly his denial of Jesus, the error
which led him the length of persecuting the holy
cause. His conversion was, therefore, surely as
it effected a practical transformation of his life,
still essentially a change of conviction. Its
basis was a 'revelation,' for such, to him, was
the appearance of Jesus. He responded to this
revelation by believing in that which it announced.

Here we find the reason why Paul the Christian
and Paul the Pharisee are not two persons, but
one. True, the direction of his effort was entirely
altered, and in the course of the new road there

was much which wrought upon him to remould his personality and readmix its elements, much that on the old way he would never have met. But the intrinsic metal of his soul remained the same—not only temperament, which indeed is hardly to be expelled by any conversion, but also the very core of character, the whole moral being.

Still it remains true, the man *as a whole* was no longer the same. All his faculties and passions received, as it were, a new soul, were seized and transfused by the new conviction, and rendered serviceable for new tasks.

2—The Chief Traits in his Religious Character

What Paul's conversion immediately brought to him was a sense, hitherto unknown, of liberation. It penetrated him to the last fibre. It breathes like a happy sigh even through the later letters— 'The old is departed ; behold, it has become new.' He knows himself freed from this whole world with its misery, its striving after nought, and the curse of its sin ; a higher world has been opened to him through Christ, and it is to him as if he already lived therein. What has his whole life been hitherto ? A bootless wrestling, a way without a goal, hard service and unfulfilled longing. But now the way leads 'from glory to glory.'

Inseparably bound up with this sense of new freedom is the consciousness that he owes all to grace. He himself can claim no share in his own transformation, not even the slightest. It is the effect of a miracle, wrought by grace. Grace laid hold of the adversary, the sinner! His own guilt forms the dark foil, against which grace shines out all the brighter. Away then with all glorying ! God and Christ are all, man is nought. This humility is with Paul no figure of speech, but the expression of what he really feels. Of like strength are those other feelings which his experience of grace kindles within him, thankfulness and joy. They inspire him with hymns.

These are the abiding basal elements in the religious character of Paul : a new feeling of joyful, of triumphant life, a deep sense of his own powerlessness, unworthiness, and need, and a pure, personal gratitude ; still the blissful certainty of possession is twinned with a great longing, which leaps onward and upward, beyond all that has been attained, to the glory of a life which has left the earth wholly behind it. But throughout we can perceive that this man is conscious of standing in real contact with the supersensible world. He does not speak like one who knows about God and Christ through hearsay, but like one who has in his own person encountered them, one who has himself felt their hands upon him.

The chief part, then, of Paul's life lay within ; and this inner life it is that glows through his letters. Not that he is at all the man to repose and revel in his own sensations. Among all the gifts with which nature had endowed him the foremost was a will as tenacious as it was keen. If only on that account he must be, after his conversion as before it, a man of deeds, as active for the gospel as he had been against it. The very depth of feeling which possessed his soul supplied strong impulses to this activity, among them, beyond doubt, the longing to atone. And so his life becomes, in truth, labour, toil, and strife.

It is astounding how he carries through plan

after plan, sets out to conquer one piece of ground after another for his cause, confirms a wavering hold, settles small questions with the whole power of his mind and yet does not forget great ones, directs and sets to with his own hand, grasps the near and the far alike, and never shows a trace of languor. But this activity appears still greater when we measure the endless renunciations and sacrifices which it demands. Hunger and thirst, all the distresses and perils of toilsome, long, dangerous journeys, shipwreck, prison, stripes, violence which threatened even his life, bitterest hatreds, and besides all this the burden of his daily labour—all this he had undergone at a time[1] when many a heavy hour still lay before him; and none of it had been able to destroy his energy or to shake his joy. Perhaps there is no other feature in the character of this man—if it is right to call it a ' feature '—so worthy of admiration as this power of self-sacrifice, just as there is little in his letters to be compared with the words in which he describes his sufferings.[2] If Christianity in general has

[1] II Cor. 11²³ sqq.
[2] I Cor. 4⁹ sqq. II Cor. 4⁷ sqq. ; 6⁴ sqq.

ennobled suffering, Paul has certainly his share in this work. He is, leaving his end out of the question, the great, typical martyr, who walks barefoot over thorns, feels them and heeds them not, or rather glories in them proudly, because they are one earnest more of the glory that shall be, and because they bring to light the law that weakness and death do but give scope to the power of God, and so are strength and life.

No one can doubt that an effect like this is born of a genuine, deep devotion to the cause, and an ever-flowing enthusiasm. Nevertheless, those who dissect motives will take account in Paul of another, a personal one. He was not free from a certain ambition—coloured by religion, no doubt, but still ambition. Abreast of all his real humility towards God there goes a certain self-consciousness which has very little in common with ordinary modesty, though it is not to be confused with vanity. He has, it must be owned, ' laboured more abundantly than they all ' ; but he knows it, too. He is keenly concerned for the amount and sum of his own achievement. He is eager to earn especial merit in the eyes of God. He claims it as his right as an apostle to be maintained by the communities. His renunciation of this right, and his maintenance of himself by his own hands, constitutes for him an especial ' glory ' which surpasses what could be required of him ; and he declares with emphasis that he would rather give up his life than this glory.[1] Such thoughts may often have played a part in his heroic endeavours. We must not be offended with their presence in the preacher of grace. What has the yard-measure of a narrow logic to do with such a personality ? The heavenly reward never loses its significance for Paul. It is the old Pharisee that here comes clearly into view. And after all, this ambition may easily be over-emphasized. It is a collateral, subsidiary motive, not more.

There is something else much more important, fundamental indeed for the appreciation of his whole work and so of the man himself. Paul felt himself bound, in duty bound by a special divine commission.

This belief in his vocation engendered another kind of egoism, stronger than the more private

[1] I Cor. 9$^{14-18}$.

sense of his own achievement, which it envelops
or dissolves into itself. It asserts itself most
strongly when he has to defend his cause and
person against opponents.[1] But it is always
present. Its tenour is that he is an apostle,
particularly predestined[2] by God himself to be a
messenger of the gospel, and furnished with power
for the task : not the only apostle, but the equal
of every other, and also uniquely entrusted with
a unique task, the mission to the heathen. In
this matter Paul is really conscious of no decision
of his own, only of the divine command, and
this is the accomplishment of the grace which
he has received : the persecutor is not only
transformed, but is planted by God as a pillar
of his cause. This gives him the proud sense of
a peculiar dignity and special rights, the sense
too that he is set up as a type and example,[3]
even though he makes no claim to have a new
Christianity. And another effect which it has
is to fuse together into a single whole the cause
and the man. The man becomes a part of the
cause. Towards God and his behest Paul's

---

[1] Cf. Gal., II Cor.   [2] Gal. 1[15].   [3] Cf. e.g., I Cor. 4[16], 11[1].

attitude is, in fact, simply that of a servant.
But it may still be that the cause covers and
justifies, now and then, the assertion of his own
personality and its claims.

If we go by his own account[1] this consciousness
of vocation was felt in its fulness from the beginning. The very moment of his conversion had
shown him that he was ordained, not simply to
the apostolate, but to the apostolate of the
Gentiles. But this looks like a slight self-deception. From a psychological point of view the
perception, at such a moment, of so specific a
vocation, is hardly comprehensible. The per-
spective of memory is apt to foreshorten and
bring together events which were originally
separate, if only there is some intrinsic connexion
between them. In any case the recognition of
his life-work had been an effect of the appearance
of Christ. On the other hand his title to the
apostolic dignity was, for him as well as for
other men, that he had ' seen ' Jesus as truly as
any apostle who had lived in his society.

It was but a short step to the idea that Christ

[1] The passages Gal. 1[16], Rom. 15[15] sq. seem to have this
meaning.

had himself, at that same time, called him to his office. If so, the sense of his own apostolic authority which breathes through his letters was also of gradual growth. But this was in any case to be expected. Until there were successes to witness for him, communities to bear united testimony, in no uncertain tones, to his vocation for this work, a crowd of helpers under his command, he could hardly have been so securely conscious of his own dignity as we find him.

In any case it remains true—Paul was very soon sure that it was his task to work for Christ ; and it is certain that, quite as soon, he interpreted the extraordinary grace done him in the Apparition as a divine induction into this calling. And nothing can be more certain than that the thought of duty definitely appointed him was a lever whose power over his active faculties increased more and more.

* * * * * * *

The second letter to the Corinthians contains (chap. 12) a unique passage. Paul describes, in few but telling strokes, a single moment of his religious life. It is again a vision. He once felt

himself caught up 'to the third heaven,' yea,
into Paradise; or rather, as he believes, he was
actually caught up thither, and there heard words
such as the lips of man may not utter. He lost
consciousness of his bodily existence. He knew not
whether it was 'in the body or out of the body.'
It is the complete picture of an ecstatic rapture.

It cannot be doubted that this hour marks
an especial climax in his life. He must look
back fourteen years to find anything so extraordinary to record. Nor can it be doubted that
he had often experienced other 'visions' and
'revelations,'[1] even if they were often no more
than dreams. His own reflections transformed
themselves into revelations, and the revelations
actuated him to new resolves. He was no stranger
to states of ecstasy in divine worship; they
belonged to that 'speaking with tongues' in
which he was an adept.[2] Consistently with all
this the apostle believes in his own—at least
momentary—inspiration; he believes that he
receives intimations of a marvellous kind from
'the Spirit.'[3]

---

[1] II Cor. 12[1]; Gal. 2[1]; Acts 27[23] sq.   [2] I Cor. 14[18].

[3] I Cor. 2[6] sqq.

All this must be taken into account, especially when we reflect how fundamental a significance, affecting his whole life, was exercised by one vision, the first. We see here that religious feeling has been heightened into enthusiasm, and Paul stands revealed as the brother of all those illuminati and visionary enthusiasts who were so highly esteemed during the Reformation, and even to-day emerge at times among the sects. He who undergoes such experiences may perhaps do great things; his religion, at least, is alive and aglow; and surely the longings, the agitation and strife which take the form of ecstasy need not, merely because they do take this form, lose a jot of their nobility: but nevertheless we feel that the form itself is something morbid. There is something which cannot be severed from this kind of religious experience—self-deception; and if it is not always dangerous, it certainly is so sometimes. A man's own thought, or the mirroring of some event in his own soul, is treated by him as a revelation. A predilection, too, for abnormal exaltations is easily engendered: though we certainly cannot impute it to Paul.

The apostle's susceptibility to visions was connected with his bodily organization, with his strong nervous excitability. It is true, of course, that ecstasy and the belief in visions were so far characteristic of the whole primitive Christian community that a special explanation in any single case may seem unnecessary. If we would form a historical conception and estimate of Paul we must not for a moment forget that fact. But he himself, in his description of the Great Vision, mentions something which forces upon us the conclusion that he was more susceptible than others to visionary experiences.

He refers to a severe trouble, which seems to him the work of some evil, demoniacal power ; a ' thorn in the flesh ' has been given him, the angel of Satan buffets him.[1] In spite of his supplications this trouble does not leave him, but recurs as before. Its connexion with his ecstasies appears in this, that he piously interprets it as a divine warning that he should not be puffed up by such lofty revelations.

A morbid trait is here clearly depicted. Paul,

---

[1] II Cor. 12⁷ sqq.

like other great historical figures—for instance, Cæsar and Napoleon—suffered from epileptic fits. This is more than suspicion ; for the apostle's description agrees with the fact that epileptics are often found subject to visions. The delight in the beholding of sublime scenes, the loss of bodily consciousness, the seizure with its convulsions and pains, form one single pathological process. Was what happened on the way to Damascus something of this kind ? We cannot be sure ; but at least this throws a peculiar light upon the nature and origin of that first vision.

To pass these things by in silence would be to obliterate an essential feature in the portrait of the man as a whole. It is probable that if we could estimate more certainly this element of morbid excitability in his nature, we should better understand his character in many respects. But exaggeration is evil. The preponderating impression which Paul makes is that of health. There speaks indeed in his letters a sensibility which is rich in emotion, and subject to sudden revulsions of mood ; his piety has a fervour which often partakes of the passionate ; his religious utterance is sometimes very high-wrought ; but in all this there is nothing *exalté*, nothing that betrays the flickering unrest of a sick soul. And our sources afford us pictures such as make us utterly forget Paul the Visionary. Who thinks of such a being, as he observes the collected wisdom and practical skill with which Paul handles the manifold problems of the Corinthian community? or when he reads the description of his voyage, the most vivid piece of narrative in the New Testament?[1] In this passage the personality of the Master has been brought, it is true, by the admiration of a fellow-traveller, too prominently into the foreground; but still we can clearly recognize that in the confusion of shipwreck it was not merely by his prophesyings, but by his superior calmness and good sense that Paul compelled the respect even of the heathen crew. There were, in fact, strong elements in his character which set a dam against the overflow of visionary fanaticism; chief of these was his tense will, but besides this his keen eye for the actual things in his field of view, and his power of intelligent thinking.

* * * * * * * *

[1] Acts 27.

The religious individuality of the apostle has its other side—if you will, its pre-condition, which is at all events indissolubly bound up with it—in a certain attitude towards the things and relations of the life of the natural world. He says indeed, ' All things are yours,' but he certainly does not mean to express a disposition of open receptiveness towards the world.[1] In this point he may be called the opposite of Luther —with whom, indeed, his affinity is very limited— but closely related to certain types of pietism.

His attitude towards particular things is that of indifference, passing here and there into aversion and enmity, and toward the world as a whole that of pessimism.

For him worldly joys do not exist. The lilies of the field and the fowls of the heaven are nothing to him. In a townsman of the ancient world this is not to be wondered at. But he never shews a gleam of sympathy with the nobler fruits of culture. He certainly despised worldly science, wherever he chanced to meet it ; the very note of the divine wisdom is that it is not comprehended

[1] I Cor. 3[21] sq.

by the understanding.[1] Work for goods and chattels is nothing to him ; we ought to have as if we had not. He knows no family life, and does not feel any privation, rather a gift of grace, in the fact that he has no inclination towards marriage. The single state would indeed always be the ideal state, if human nature did not make it inadvisable for most people.[2] Civic independence is little to him ; a slave who is a Christian ought not to wish to be other than a slave, even if he can become free.[3] But in the world in general and in its life he sees only the nothingness, the sickness, the ruin wrought by sin. The gloom of his view of the world would be even more marked, if the joy of redemption did not shed so bright a gleam over his letters.

These thoughts are certainly not caused only by the belief that the end of the world is at hand ; his estimate of marriage, for instance, cannot be so explained. In his view the married man, in giving his heart to his wife, withdraws it from the Lord ; only the celibate preserves his purity unimpaired.[4] Not all his views, however, are

---

[1] I Cor. 1[16] sqq.   [2] I Cor. 7[1, 7, 8].   [3] I Cor. 7[21].
[4] I Cor. 7[32] sqq.

ascetic, like this. They cannot be explained in any satisfactory degree by particular experiences or observations of the pagan world. They spring rather out of his entire absorption in his religion, which leaves no room for worldly interests. Religion is everything to him, and therefore the rest is nothing. But, although this is a feature of the man's most personal individuality, it must nevertheless be connected with a mood which was, in his time, of general prevalence. The Jewish apocalyptic writings, such as IV Ezra, breathe a weariness of the world and of existence in it which stands in the closest affinity to that of Paul. This pessimism had its representatives too in paganism. The philosophy of life which the so-called Cynics—who were rather preachers, influenced by Stoic thinking, than philosophers— brought into the streets and alleys, affords a striking parallel.

3—The Moral Self of the Man

The nature of Paul's religion comes out unmistakably in his letters. Warmth and depth of feeling, strength and enthusiasm, the direct freshness of his religious experience and its exclusive dominance over him, all unite to stamp him as specifically, and in the highest sense, a religious nature. May we in a similar sense go on to speak of him as a specifically ethical personality ? We doubt it; though we must certainly assign to Paul as his due a high place among the great moral characters.

A deep moral earnestness pervades every one of his letters. He knows no other God than him who hates sin and commands goodness. A pure life is to him a part of religion. His ethical writings contain, beyond question, many evidences of a finely developed moral feeling. He who can require that, out of consideration for the brother who does not feel so free as ourselves, we should forgo even permissible things, he who again lays down the principle that we should avoid the permissible, so long as our moral conviction, our conscience, does not give the fullest assent to its enjoyment,[1] must have possessed a fine moral feeling. And who can doubt that what Paul preached to others he tried, in the simplest, fullest sense, to practise in his own life ? Long

---

[1] I Cor. 8⁷ sqq. Rom. 14¹³ sqq. ²³ sq.

ago, in the Pharisaic school of the law, he had learned to deal conscientiously with himself, to rein his will, to set rules for himself, to hold himself under observation. All that belongs to the domain of ' sanctification,' that is of self-discipline, must have had its roots there. And he had never been negligent in this matter. He was the runner who strives for the prize.

But the recognition of ideals is not a perfectly safe standard for the actual life; least of all, the recommendation of rules which belong only to the traditional ideal of virtue. A man may strive to avoid the faults he recognizes, without really having a full knowledge of himself. Religious enthusiasm is no guarantee against human weaknesses; it may even give occasion to some. And sanctification, the mastery over base impulses, does not always ensure those moral values which are decisive in the relation of man to man.

In any case it is somewhat difficult to present a full portrait, without omitting the finer features, of the moral individuality of Paul. Letters reveal the personality of their author, but also conceal it. For even when they are as free

from pose and artificiality as those of Paul, still
they present a personality always in the light
in which it sees itself, and in which it wishes
to be seen. Moreover, an active character like
Paul can only be clearly recognized in its activity.
But what do we see of the activity of Paul ?
Several rough outlines of the form it outwardly
took, very much of the religious spirit which
inspired it, but little of his behaviour in definite
situations, his concrete relations to men and
things, and yet it is only in these that the real
moral character of active transactions comes
clearly to light. We have practically no contemporary verdict either on the man or his doings.
Where do we read what Peter, what Barnabas
thought of the man who pressed before them,
and came into no gentle collision with them ?
It would be an interesting piece of knowledge.

* * * * * * * *

Paul glories, not without reason, in his work
in the communities : ' Who is weak, and I am not
weak ? Who is offended, and I burn not ? '[1]
He possessed a rich power of love, ready for

[1] II Cor. 11.29.

unceasing service, was capable of soft emotions, and could speak in tones as tender as they were fervent. Even in the harsh letter to the Galatians there is one passage of this kind.[1] But the most beautiful testimony is borne by the epistle to the Philippians. Still we do not receive the impression of an exceptional natural kindness, an indefeasible benevolence towards mankind as such. It was not every community which showed him such trust, affection, and faithful solicitude as that of Philippi. And these were conditions of his love. It flowed out towards the friends of his cause, the objects of his mission, whom he might strive to gain, those already won, for whom he might labour and sacrifice himself. It was genuine, warm-hearted, personal love, but was nevertheless determined, or partly determined, by other than purely human considerations. When people go their own way, will not yield to him or even oppose him, he is ready enough to deal with them, even if he seems equally ready to pardon.[2] He often grows incensed, becomes rough, harsh, and bitter, and makes use of irony,

[1] Gal. 4[12] sqq.   [2] II Cor. 2[5] sqq.

of which he is a master.[1] Peter's behaviour at
Antioch he bluntly dubs—not altogether without
justification—hypocrisy.[2] Those whom he attacks,
however, with the whole force and passion of
his nature are his personal adversaries, the Jewish-
Christian teachers, who opposed him in his own
communities, especially in Galatia and Corinth.
He curses them roundly, calls them false apostles,
deceitful labourers, servants of Satan, who wear
the mask of servants of righteousness—he even
abuses them as ' dogs.'[3] No doubt, even Paul
the convert would have been capable of violently
persecuting such foes, and the apostates too,
as enemies of God, if he had only had the power.

His wrath against these people is, moreover,
easy to understand. They threatened the work
for which he lived, had brought confusion into
his communities, and had not been sparing of
complaints and the sowing of suspicions against
himself. Towards such people he could not, of
course, take up a purely objective and impartial
attitude. But he paints them altogether too
black. There can be no serious doubt that those

---

[1] II Cor. 11[16-22], 10 ; I Cor. 4[8] sqq.   [2] Gal. 2[13].
[3] Gal. 1[8] sq ; II Cor. 11[13] sqq ; Phil. 3[2].

zealots of the law were also trying to serve a
cause, that from their standpoint they believed
that genuine Christianity was endangered by the
teaching of the innovator, Paul. But from the
apostle we learn nothing of this. He imputes
to them only personal, self-seeking, base, and
hateful motives; they only desired by their
zeal for the law to curry favour with the Jews,
and escape the persecution which the cross of
Christ brings with it.[1] There is another case
in which the justice of his verdict is at least
very questionable.[2] While the apostle lay im-
prisoned in Rome some Christians, who clearly
would have nothing to do with Paul, carried
on missionary work there. Paul speaks of them
with the utmost bitterness; unfortunately we
have not their defence. He actually says that
their real object is not to make Christ known,
but only to inflict on Paul himself the distress
which their preaching causes him. True, he
adds a magnanimous sounding word, by which
he seems to lift himself above the personal controversy: 'What matters it? In this way or that,

---

[1] Gal. 6[12] sq. cf. II Cor. 10-13.　　[2] Phil. 1[15] sqq. cf. 2[21].

D

with or without guileful intent, Christ is made
known, and I rejoice at it.' But that is only a
kind of resignation, through which the bitterness
of his mood can still be seen.

What the apostle's opponents said against him
may partly be gathered from the allusions in his
letters. Here, then, for once, we may be said
to hear the voices of contemporaries. He was
charged with cowardice : when he was present,
they said, he was humble and weak, but at a
distance, in his letters, he was stern and high-
spoken ; moreover, he extolled and glorified
himself, put himself forward in the community
as the ruler of belief, was double-tongued, wavering in his plans, wrote otherwise than as he
thought, and tried to make himself popular.[1]
His renunciation of the right to be supported by
the community was interpreted to mean that he
did not consider himself a genuine apostle ;
besides, he was cunning enough to plunder the
community all the same, by laying hands on
the money which they raised by collection.[2]

[1] II Cor. 10^1 sq. $^{10, 8}$; 1^{24}, 12-23. Gal. 1^{10} (cf. also I Thess.
2^5, ' flattery ').
[2] II Cor. 11^{10} ; 12^{16} ; 7^2.

The odiousness of these aspersions, especially those that impugn his honesty, is obvious. But little as they can be used as an index of Paul's general character, there may still be a germ of truth in one or other of the strokes—for instance, in the matter of self-glorification. At any rate, his letters contain traces of a certain pliancy, we might almost say tactic, which offered a handle to unfavourable interpretation. In one case that seems to us to be especially clear.

When the apostle was in Macedonia and Greece he laid the greatest weight on the making of a collection for the community in Jerusalem. It was to speak in his favour in that community. In order that the impression might be considerable the collection must be great. He devoted two whole chapters to this object in the second Corinthian letter.[1] But anyone who reads without prepossession and pierces through the edifying phraseology to the kernel of the matter—it is sometimes necessary to discount Paul's edifying formulas and flourishes—will hardly gain a pleasant impression. Here speaks, perhaps un-

[1] II Cor. 8 and 9.

consciously, a tactician, who understands men and does not shrink from going a little bit round-about to reach his goal. In all ways, with strong allusions, for instance, to the heavenly usury, he tries to make the collection acceptable to his readers ; and, since he is not quite sure of them, he interlards his appeal with forced eulogies ; he even extols their readiness to give, although we can clearly see that he himself does not really believe in it.[1]

We must not exaggerate this element in Paul ; but one who can write in this way says a word too much in other cases too, in order to gain some end —uses little artifices, colours and accommodates a little. A certain amount of calculation might even be found in the short letter in which Paul seeks to induce Philemon, a Christian of high standing in Colossæ, to receive with kindness a runaway slave, whom Paul has in the interval converted, or—still better—to send him back to be Paul's assistant. The little piece does show insurpassably how this man, finely organized to the last ounce of his being, understands the art

[1] II Cor. 8[7], [24] ; 9[2-5].

of working upon the will of others. Still, ' calculation' is here an inapplicable expression ; it is
much too coarse a word. The art of persuasion
uses in this case none but acceptable and kindly
means. This little note, with its mixture of
cordiality and politeness, trust and reserve, has
a quite unusual charm. It is the finest piece
of this kind from Paul's hand that we possess.

It cannot but appear astonishing that such a
man did not possess any absolute sovereignty
over the hearts of the members of his communities.
In Corinth, as well as in Galatia, he was condemned
from time to time to see great segments turn
away from him, until it became a question if
any would be left. The causes were certainly
in part external to his personality, but perhaps
lay partly within it. His appearance was not
very imposing ; there were some too who could
not tolerate the blunt force and stern severity
with which he set himself against moral laxity
or disturbances of the life of the community ;
but apart from all this, he does not really seem—
winning as he could be and often was—to have
had a wholly loveable nature. His status in
his own communities was nevertheless that of a

master. He was accustomed to carry out his own will and force it upon others ; he laid claim to the authority of an apostle, was always right, and always ready to show his rough side to the less docile members. Such a man naturally gains crowds of reverent admirers, and devoted secretaries, eager to serve him ; but he repels and alienates those who do not like coercion.

* * * * * * * *

Enough of details. He whom we have sketched is no saint, but a man. Edification would cover up such a figure with a conventional, monotonous, neutral tint, that of the ideal Christian. This is not good. Paul had some real weaknesses, perhaps more than we see. They are, as it seems, the frailties of one who, possessing a passionate, excitable temperament, identifies his own person wholly with the will of God ; or shall we say of one who lives for an end, and measures all men and all things by their relation to that end ? The more humane virtues of reasonableness and fairness, of magnanimity, tolerance, and respect for every personal right, and that kind of rectitude to which the slight distortions and the more innocent arts of an instinctive diplomacy are strange—such virtues in such a man are easily overborne. They did not constitute the strength of Paul. But it is due to him to remember that they did not constitute the strength of Christianity in that age ; in hortatory discourses, not only in those of Paul, they take no prominent place.

But these are in reality only weaknesses, not stains. They are the defects incident to his virtues. And Paul is able to bear their exposure. The very fact that he wholly identifies himself with God's cause, and devotes his whole glowing soul to one dominating purpose, justifies a claim that he shall be judged from this standpoint; and then every question of the purity of his actual will, the sincerity of his innermost self, falls to the ground.

The sharpest contrasts were united in this richly endowed nature. Pertinacious and impulsive, turbulent and stable, inconsiderate and tender, in his intolerance bitter to the point of hardness and acrimony, and yet a man of soft sensibility ; unyielding and yet pliant ; all enthusiasm and glow, all sober prudence ; a thinker, a meditator, and yet even more a restless

toiler—no scheme will suffice to comprehend
the whole man. His character is far from being
reducible to that harmony which can be allotted
to more tranquil souls. But one spirit breathes
through it all : it is permeated by the one great
thought of his life, which arises out of his religion.
For this he toils, sacrifices, strives, lives, and
dies. And so he remains not merely a great,
but a noble character ; a faithful steward, to his
very depths an unselfish fighter, and a true hero.

II

HIS LIFE WORK

1—The Mission and its Conduct

PAUL was not the only missionary to the Gentiles of his time ; by his side there were others working independently, if sometimes in touch with him. Moreover, he was not the first missionary to the Gentiles. To all appearance the beginning was made by unknown men from Cyprus and Cyrene. Driven from Jerusalem by the persecution to which Stephen fell a victim, they preached to ' the Greeks ' in the cosmopolitan city of Antioch in Syria[1] : this notice in the Acts of the Apostles can hardly be set aside. Barnabas entered upon this work before Paul ; for at the outset his relation to Paul is clearly that of the

---

[1] Acts 11[19] sqq. According to Acts 10 Peter would have taken the first step. This is incorrect.

elder and prior worker.[1] He was perhaps of
more importance than we know, and it required a
fairly long stretch of time before his comrade
Paul surpassed him.

And yet the tradition is not so far wrong in
making all the rest disappear behind Paul. He
remains the one decisive man. It is not only the
greatness of his labour and of his success ; he
was also the first to give solidity and clearness
to the Gentile mission, by winning for it a recognised right to exist ; he inspired it with a great,
far-reaching impulse, and supplied it with a mighty
rousing example.

How did he become a missionary to the Gentiles ?
As to this we have no serviceable information—if,
that is, we refuse to date its beginning from the
very hour of his conversion. He certainly began
to preach in the first three years after his conversion, which were divided between ' Arabia ' and
Damascus. For he was obliged to quit Damascus as a fugitive.[2] But had he then already
preached to Gentiles ? It is by no means improbable that he first worked within Judaism,

[1] Observe the order of the names in Acts 13[1, 2] ; 14[14].
[2] II Cor. 11[33] sq. ; Acts 9[20-25].

and entered on the new path for the first time in Antioch.

* * * * * * * *

It is usual to present the progress of the Pauline mission in the scheme of the three great journeys, which led back each time either to Antioch or Jerusalem. But this is unsatisfactory, if only because Paul had already been at work as a missionary many years before the first journey. Besides, in the later time Antioch did not really remain the fixed basis of his missionary expeditions. Certain points in his ministry, especially Ephesus, were made a sort of basis for longer or shorter excursions.

In surveying the whole the first and most important point is to distinguish two phases and two chief fields of missionary work. The three years that followed the conversion are here left out of account.

The first epoch, which embraces fully fourteen years,[1] had its scene laid in Syria, more particularly Antioch, and the neighbouring land which was Paul's home, Cilicia. It is more than

[1] Gal. 2¹; 1¹⁸, ²¹; 2¹¹. According to another interpretation, eleven years.

probable, but still no more than conjecture, that
Tarsus itself played a great part in this ministry ;
but the great work which was done in this region
is involved in the deepest obscurity. According
to the Acts[1] that ' first ' journey with Barnabas,
which led to Cyprus and certain regions of Asia
Minor, falls into this period.

The second period, which ends with the im-
prisonment of Paul (58 or 59 A.D.), is only about
half as long, and yet is by far the more important.
The area of work extends itself northwards,
but its chief tendency is towards the west, and
so for the first time really into the actual world
of Græco-Roman culture. Paul treads Euro-
pean soil ; he works in Macedonia and Greece
('Achæa '). Parts of Asia Minor come also into
the field : the inland district of Galatia,[2] and
those strips of the west coast which made up
the Roman province of ' Asia '—in later days a
singularly important seat of Christianity. In

[1] Acts 13 and 14. It is difficult to make out what significance this journey could have with relation to the work
in Syria and Cilicia.

[2] Many scholars take the Galatia of Paul to have been
only the southern districts of what is properly called Galatia—
Pisidia, Lycaonia.

Asia Ephesus, in Europe Corinth was the most important foundation.

From Antioch to Thessalonica and Corinth, even to Illyria[1]—that is no small piece of the world as it then was. Still it would be easy to form exaggerated ideas. The Christian language is fond of hyperbole—such as that Macedonia has received the word of God, or that the gospel ' has been made known to all the world.'[2] This was the speech of those who worked and believed : but the reality had another face. The activity of Paul was very far from comprising those regions in their whole breadth and depth. The country districts do not come into question at all, except perhaps in Syria. The mission was concerned with the towns, and almost alone with the more important places on the great trade roads. These traced out Paul's routes for him. This explains the preponderance of coast districts among his halting-places.

The success, however, of the preaching in these several places was not, in the eyes of a cool contemporary observer, very important. The

[1] Rom. 15[19].   [2] e.g., Col. 1[23].

whole work of Paul aroused public attention
hardly more than that of a gifted and fiery
sectarian preacher in a large city of to-day, who
becomes known through collisions with the
police or similar disturbances. If in any one
great city a hundred or a hundred and fifty
people were won, this was certainly a quite
unusual measure of success. This is no dis-
paragement of Paul's work. If a hundred persons
are somewhere near a hundred active forces, if
three or four towns in a province are so many
centres of a swiftly growing movement, that is
not so little. And in any case the building up
of a small but firmly cemented community in
regions which lie so far apart is an extraordinary
performance for one man. Our admiration, however, is chiefly aroused by the bold forward pressure
of the second period.

The mission of Paul seems at that time to
have been seized by a new spirit. It shows itself
in his swift passage from district to district,
and in that bold plan of the apostle's[1] to go by
way of Rome to the western boundary of the

---

[1] Rom. 15²³ sq. ²⁸.

world, to Spain, and to work there. He who could charge himself with such a purpose had not hitherto been merely groping his way, or letting himself be driven by occasion from point to point—often as that must have been the case, especially at first—but he had also proceeded by plan and with a connected scheme. The one appropriate name for this mission is indeed, then, a ' world-mission ' ; the gospel shall, within a short space of time, be carried to all nations, and the chief part of the work falls to the apostle. That his course was abruptly broken off—we can hardly believe that he had ever reached Spain —does not affect the breadth of his thought.

A plan like this has for us something fantastic, something even bizarre about it. Paul looked forward to the speedy coming of the end of the world. He could not count much, therefore, on the slow extension of his faith from the centres it had gained. Why then this roaming into the distance ? Was the work in Galatia finished ? Did not the neighbouring regions offer rich and much more convenient fields ? It appears that his ultimate thoughts took less account of the number of persons won, and of particular places,

than of whole lands and provinces. If the name
of Christ were only preached in every province,
then the whole world—which meant in effect,
for Paul, the Roman empire—would have heard
the gospel. Looking at things thus we can easily
see how so great a spur to action as the approaching end of the world would drive him on a swift
quest of new fields of preaching.

The reason why Paul, in the first place, came
to leave his narrower range of activity in Syria
and Cilicia, and spread his wings for a long flight,
has to do with those discussions in Jerusalem
and Antioch in which he stood for the right of
his Gentile mission, and at last came into collision
with Peter and Barnabas. He relied thenceforward more upon himself. The more exact
workings of the matter are unknown to us.

* * * * * * * *

According to the Acts of the Apostles it was
Paul's regular habit to preach first to the Jews,
and not to claim the right of going to the Gentiles
until the Jews had unmistakably rejected his
message.[1] This is a remarkable rule for a man

---

[1] e.g., Acts 13^{46}.

to follow who knew himself specially commissioned
to the Gentiles! In fact it is incredible. In
rejecting, however, this regular scheme we do
not necessarily reject the positive statements
according to which Paul did actually make a
beginning in the Jewish synagogues. They are
perhaps deserving of more acceptance than
criticism has generally accorded them. If he
says of himself that he has been to the Jews a
Jew, in order to win Jews,[1] this practice is not
so astonishing, and, looked into a little more
closely, appears to be even a condition of his
success.

The Judaism of the Dispersion was derided,
mocked, and hated throughout the civilized world,
and yet exercised on many circles a strong attrac-
tion. On its own side it had devoted effort to
the task of winning ground. By means of a
propaganda which may be regarded as a half
prefiguration of the Christian mission it had
attached to itself in all places crowds of proselytes
and 'worshippers of God.' The different grades
of these were very numerous, and reached from

[1] I Cor. 9²⁰.

E

simple attendants at the synagogue to Jews in the fullest sense.

This state of things offered great advantages to Paul. By trying to enter into relations with the Jews, among whom he could, of course, most easily establish a connexion and gain a starting-point, by speaking as a Jew in the synagogue, he was taking the best way to introduce his religion into a city. It appeared as a variety of a faith which had long aroused interest. But the chief point is that in the Gentile adherents of Judaism he found a public which was prepared, if any was prepared, for his preaching, and which at the same time made a bridge for him to the pagan circles proper. Much in that age combined to level the way for the new faith. What did not the one fact alone mean to the missionary, that the Greek language was everywhere understood and spoken ? But there was hardly any other thing so important as the great work of preparation which Judaism had done, and which could now be simply made use of.

Judaism avenged itself, and indemnified itself for the unwilling assistance which it had rendered the apostle, by long drawn out obstruction and

even persecution. To the Jews he was not merely
the apostate, the proclaimer of an accursed faith ;
he was also the troublesome intruder, the rival
who fished in their pool. Paul had to bear the
traces of their rage literally on his body. Five
times, he himself relates, he underwent the
punishment of flogging.[1] And everywhere the
attempts were repeated to infuriate the rabble
against him, or by means of denunciations to
embroil him with the authorities.

* * * * * * * *

It was not by elegance and polish of speech
that Paul wrought upon his hearers. He himself
was conscious of a lack in this respect.[2] It was
indeed not a real defect ; rhetorical garnishings,
however agreeable to the enlightened, could
only detract from the power of the gospel.[3]
But the reader of his letters will judge the apostle's
power of speech more favourably than he did
himself. He who, while dictating, can attain
such movement and fire, can storm along with
his thoughts so victoriously, must as a speaker
have possessed something which drew the hearers

[1] II Cor. 11²⁴.   [2] I Cor. 2³ ; II Cor. 11⁶.
[3] I Cor. 2⁴ sq.

under his spell and chained them to his discourse. And this discourse—what was it ? How did Paul the missionary proffer his gospel ?

We can easily outline its setting forth to the Jews. The character of the preaching to the Gentiles is a harder question. Our answer depends partly on the conception we form of the public to which the apostle addressed himself.

His adherents belonged, as is well known, preponderantly to the lower and poorer classes : chiefly women and slaves, small tradesmen too, and operatives ; no peasants. But what interests us here is the religious condition of this public.

The age of Paul, as a whole, cannot be considered irreligious or hostile to religion. Many powers were certainly at work in the overthrow of polytheism. But this movement went on chiefly among the upper classes ; and it is important to recognise that a peculiar, new religious life was emerging, and laying ever firmer hold upon the world ; the religions of the Orient had begun their campaign of conquest in the Græco-Roman world, and this revival was a result of it. The old combined with the new in innumerable forms. This is the time of ' Syncretism,' of the

mixture of religions. The new element consisted
chiefly in the longing for redemption. The thought
of the world to come was a living reality ; people
sought after purity and ' regeneration,' redemption
from the finite, redemption to eternal life, and
asked after the way of redemption. This way
was shown to them in mysteries and cults. The
' initiation '—we should say, the sacrament—
played a great part ; it imparted ' life,' or gave
security for its possession. He who had been
received by the mysterious rite into the religious
community felt himself redeemed. This is no
exhaustive picture. There was also a decided
tendency towards asceticism and renunciation
of the world, longing for a revelation, and other
elements.

Many a heathen, it is certain, found Christianity
congenial chiefly because of its opposition to
belief in the gods. It met half-way the criticism
and enlightenment which had grown up within
paganism itself—positively phrased, the directly
monotheistic tendency of the times. But it is
clear that quite other things were able to attract.
The Christian thought of eternal life, and its
converse, the idea of the dreadful judgment,

the belief in redemption through Christ, holy
scripture with its infallible divine oracles, all
found important points of attachment awaiting
them. In especial the sacred acts were a direct
recommendation of the new religion, which also
was oriental: baptism as 'initiation,' and the
Lord's Supper as a pendant to the numerous
solemn meals of the cults.[1]

All this must be held in mind if we are to form
a conception of the real missionary preaching
of Paul and also of its effect. His letters, which
are all addressed to people already won and
instructed, do not help us directly to an idea of it.

The emphatic assertion of belief in one God,
and criticism of polytheism, which must have
held an important place in the preaching, have
in the letters fallen quite into the background.
In these matters Paul was treading exactly in
the footsteps of the Jews. His thoughts were
not those of an historian of religion; he had no
eye at all for the characteristic qualities of various
religions. Like a true Jew he drew a simple and
broad distinction between Judaism and the

[1] I Cor. 10[14-22].

religion of the 'Gentiles,' which was, without
distinction, darkness and destruction. His dark
picture of it[1] is painted altogether with conventional Jewish colours. As a preacher then
he must have brought the ordinary Jewish polemic
to bear against the idols of wood and stone,
against the vicious and bestial gods, and he
certainly did not hide his belief that behind these
pretended gods there lurked hostile and frightful
demons. In this connexion he pointed to the
witness borne by creation to one God and Creator.[2]

It would however be false to suppose that he
must have begun directly with these things,
and suppressed for a time what was specifically
Christian, in the interests of a rational pedagogic
system of instruction. In truth it would neither
have been rational nor worthy of a pedagogue to
preach the rational, even if he had attached
any particular value to this point of view. What
people sought in religion—leaving cultured circles
out of account—was by no means the rational :
they were perfectly ready to accept mystic

---

[1] Rom. 1[18] sqq. The 'Wisdom of Solomon,' in our O.T.
Apocrypha, offers parallels to almost every stroke.

[2] Rom. 1[19] sq.

ideas. And so we can see from hints in his
letters that he did not in the least shrink from
coming out at once with what was to him the
kernel of the matter. In Corinth even, in spite
of the favour in which 'philosophy,' which
meant rhetoric, stood in that city, he began
immediately with the point which was a stumbling-
block to the Gentiles, with the 'foolishness'
of the cross of Christ : in the cross lay redemption; the cross was therefore the wisdom of God.[1]

2—The Care of the Communities

A transient proclamation of the gospel was not
enough for Paul ; for him everything depended
on well-founded communities. The care which
he expends in making them such belongs to his
missionary work just as much as does his restless
journeying to new fields, and the preaching by
which he lays a first foundation.

As an organizer, a father, and—in the collective
rather than the individual sense—as guardian
of the souls of the communities, Paul extorts our
admiration.

The least part of his work lay in external

1 I Cor. 1¹⁸⁻²⁵.

regulations. What he may have done in this direction, influenced presumptively by the example of the communities of the Jewish Dispersion, must remain here undiscussed. There can hardly be any mention of a ' constitution.' The circumstances were too small and immature for that. But the teaching and building up of the communities was certainly not yet the duty of ecclesiastical officials ; it belonged as a matter of course to the hand which had thereunto received the ' gift ' of the ' spirit.'

But what an abundance of questions and tasks the inner life of the community produced ! The Jewish element, no doubt, which was everywhere to be found, was, if only as the result of the same definite type of instruction, in sympathy with the aims of the apostle, and able to give him important assistance. How different was the case of the converted heathen ! They were divided by a great gulf from many of his ethical habits and conceptions, especially in relation to the sexual life, and to sensual indulgence in general. Paul came with the strict morality of a Jew, which was too deeply in earnest to brook any abatement. The field for moral instruction was very great. The religious customs of paganism extended far and wide into the daily life of a citizen, even to the purchase of meat in the market. Is a Christian at liberty to buy and eat the flesh of sacrificial beasts which is there for sale ? May he do so when it is distinctly declared to be such ? May he go further and accept a pagan invitation to a repast, which means to partake of meat offered to an idol ?[1] Numerous practical problems occurred in married life, not only on account of mixed marriages, but also through the tendency towards asceticism. Ought a Christian wife to separate from her pagan husband ? May a Christian maiden marry a heathen ? May a widow marry again ? Is abstention from marriage to be commended ?[2] In all these connexions and many others the paths to be trodden by the Christian life had to be sought out and determined. Some of these problems may have already confronted the Judaism of the Dispersion, but for the most part they were new. Paul had therefore to construct for the first time a sort of casuistical code for

[1] I Cor. 8 ; 10¹⁴⁻²³.   [2] I Cor. 7.

the ethics of the community. To depict it **we**
should have to copy the whole picture which is
preserved in I Corinthians. The letter goes
deeply into this work of direction, decision,
adjustment, and bears splendid witness to the
circumspection, sobriety, and tact of the apostle—
most of all, to his social sense.

In Corinth[1] the converts revelled in ecstasy.
At times of service one after another would begin
to pray and exclaim in unintelligible, enraptured
words and sounds ; every one would improvise
as the spirit impelled him, and speak ' in tongues '
long before his neighbours had finished. In
such ecstatic speeches Paul recognizes a real
work of the holy spirit : but he sets himself
energetically against this kind of conduct. The
prophet, he says, who predicts, admonishes, and
comforts, is greater than the speaker with tongues ;
for he speaks intelligibly, and only intelligible
and intelligent utterances can help the community.
But high above all gifts of the spirit stands one,
which takes precedence of everything—love.[2]—
The apostle inclines, in his own personal feeling,

---

[1] I Cor. 14.   [2] I Cor. 12³¹ ; 13¹ sqq.

very much towards the ascetic view of marriage ;
but he is very far from laying it down unconditionally as a practical rule for the community.
He seems almost to repress the ascetic tendency
more than he encourages it, for he sees its dangers.
—The state of those who, through an ascetic
repulsion, avoid meat and wine,[1] or are in dread
that they might sin by partaking of sacrificial
meat,[2] he regards as mental bondage. His
principle really demands that he should refuse
to yield a step to these views, and should contend
for the utterly indifferent character of such
externals ; but in fact he urges those who feel
themselves free in such matters to resign their
freedom, if it causes offence to the 'weak'
brother.

Here we can clearly perceive how the thought
of his work has taken hold of his soul and determined even the development of his own personality.
His zeal for the community has repressed his own
ecstatic and ascetic impulses. It takes always
the first place ; the question he always asks is,
what ' builds up.' It is no mere accident that

[1] Rom. 14.   [2] I Cor. 8 ; 10²³ sqq.

we find so many exhortations to concord, peace,
brotherly love, subordination, and order. And
how fierce is his attack, when the path of regulated,
decent morality has been forsaken,[1] or when
cliques and parties—even those that vow allegiance
to himself—threaten the community with dis-
ruption ![2]

A picture stands before his eyes, an ideal of
the church, if it is not too early to speak so : a
confederacy, gathered about one Lord, harmonious
and linked firmly together, every member in its
place, every force subserving the whole,[3] moral
purity its cognizance and its glory in the midst
of a corrupt society ;[4] every smaller confederacy
feeling itself one with all its fellows near and far,
and bound by living ties to the great whole. To
help to realize this ideal is the endeavour and
solicitude of his soul. It is an ‘ ecclesiastical ’
feeling and instinct that guides him.

Paul did not toil alone. He multiplied himself
in his disciples and helpers, who were, be it
remembered, of both sexes. Silvanus, Timothy,

---

[1] I Cor. 11[2] sqq.   [2] I Cor. 1–4 ; esp. 1[18] sqq. 3[3] sqq.
[3] I Cor. 12[12] sqq. ; Rom. 12[4] sqq.
[4] e.g., I Thess. 4[12] ; I Cor. 10[32].

Titus are the most prominent, but a multitude
of other names come into the list. Of one of
these, Epaphras, we learn almost accidentally
through the epistle to the Colossians that he
had founded communities, which he placed under
the authority of Paul, in the three Phrygian cities
of Colossæ, Laodicea, and Hierapolis.

It was, of course, incidental to Paul's care for
the communities that he should visit them again.
It sometimes depended on such visits whether he
held the threads in his own hand or not. In
this connexion, however, we must also remember
the correspondence of which only a part, if an
especially important part, has come down to us.
His letters are really a part of his missionary
work, and must in this sense be read—not merely
in fragments or ' texts,' and not merely in anti-
quated translations—if we are to feel their charm.
They supply the place of Paul's personal presence,
prepare the way for his visits, and whether
rapidly written, or more deliberately laboured,
they enter directly into the active questions of
the life of the community.

* * * * * * *

3—The Fight for the Work

Even in the nascent church Paul's mission to
the Gentiles was confronted by a counter-influence
of the greatest strength. It proceeded from the
missionary views which obtained in the so-called
primitive community, that is, the Jewish Christians
of Jerusalem. These views hung like a weight
of lead about the apostle in his progress, and
forced him to a warfare in which his work was
obliged to expend much strength, but also in
reality grew stronger.

The whole picture has its very unpleasant side,
and cruelly disturbs our conception of the purely
ideal character of primitive Christian conditions.
On the other hand, under the given circumstances,
this strife may be called an historical necessity, and
here as elsewhere war was ' the father of things.'

In spite of the freedom of his attitude, Jesus
had not broken with the Mosaic law, and the
primitive community had adhered from the
beginning to the Jewish mode of life. In the
sequel its conservatism increased. It approached
somewhat nearer to ordinary Judaism. The
incipient mission to the Gentiles was what produced
a reactionary movement. The members of that

community were not indeed 'Christians'; they
regarded themselves simply as Jews who believed
in Messiah.

Jesus had not contemplated a Gentile mission.
A ministry among the heathen might nevertheless,
from the standpoint of Jerusalem, have been
developed; but then the Gentile would have
been obliged to become, wholly or in part, a Jew.
On the other hand, in the mission itself there
lay a strong incentive to discard Jewish rites.
To the pagans circumcision, and the laws about
clean and unclean foods, were obstacles pure and
simple. These customs appeared not only bizarre
and childish; they were real burdens in the
social life, exposed people to mockery, and made
division in families. Consider, for instance, the
effect alone of restriction to kosher meat.

So they stood face to face, a mission to which
freedom from the Law was the breath of life, and
a community to which the Law was a sacred
thing. How could the members of this community
treat as their equals people who did not know
what, in their eyes, was the chief requirement of
piety? This standpoint was narrow; perhaps
we are apt to-day to exaggerate its narrowness.

We must enter into the feelings, the necessary feelings, of the Jew. What would happen if a group among ourselves were to declare baptism to be not indispensable, but rather a hindrance to the gospel ?

Even though the advocate of the mission and the primitive community were knit together by the bond of the same faith, still a crisis, attended with much excitement, was hardly to be avoided ; the less because Jerusalem, as the mother society, possessed a natural authority in the feeling of all Christians. But what brought the situation to a sharp point was this, that the Gentile mission was not homogeneous : everywhere there were believing Jews by the side of the converted pagans. The two parts formed but one community. What was its practice to be ? From his point of view the Jewish Christian was forced to look upon the Gentile Christian as unclean ; he might not sit down with him—consider what that meant— to the Lord's Supper ; he might not wed a Gentile girl. It was inevitable that as the mission progressed it should lead to the alienation of Jews in heathen lands from the Law. And the resulting shock to Jewish sensibility was equally inevitable.

F

These were the lines on which the life-battle of the apostle was actually waged.

His letters show the keenest appreciation of what was at stake if the new faith was to be continuously burdened with Jewish ways of life. The clearness of his principle stamps itself unmistakably upon his theological thought. But this clearness had been reached, we must presume, step by step, and only through the experience gained in his evangelical work itself. The circumstances of his conversion, we may suppose, made the decision for this forward step easier to make. A concurrent cause of it is probably to be found in the example which was set him in the freer schools of Jewish propaganda among the Dispersion. We are not in a position to trace its development exactly.

Again, we have not even an approximation to a complete survey of the controversy. Still we are acquainted with two particular scenes, significant scenes, in its course, and a part of the efforts which were made to destroy the liberated mission.

The first scene is played in Jerusalem, and is really a kind of overture to the whole play. The two famous reports of it, the second chapter of Galatians and the fifteenth chapter of the Acts, which have set innumerable theological pens in motion, contain irreconcilable contradictions. The Acts of the Apostles has certainly distorted things a little; but also Paul's report, which is that of an eyewitness, leaves something to be wished; it contains obscurities, was written too in a passionate moment, and pursues the definite aim of establishing his independence of the apostles in Jerusalem. Perhaps there is a little heightening of the colour, for which allowance should be made; but the actual facts must be accurately recorded.

Some of the strictest zealots of the Law had come to Antioch, and observed Paul's aims and efforts on the spot. Their report—Paul's biting term for them is ' false brethren who stole in '[1]— aroused astonishment and commotion in Jerusalem. A personal explanation became necessary; Paul went with Barnabas and with Titus, who was still uncircumcised, to Jerusalem. Thus came about the discussion which has been too pompously

[1] Gal. 2⁴.

called 'the Apostolic Council.' Paul knew that
the question at issue really was whether he 'had
run in vain.'[1] It depended on the award of the
original apostles. It was fortunate for him that
he had hitherto come only into fleeting contact
with them.[2] He had had time to achieve actual
facts, before he was interfered with. It was
this actual achievement which overcame the
'pillars of the community,' James 'the Lord's
brother,' Peter, and John. They were forced
to admit not only that Paul had won Gentiles,
but that the same gifts of the spirit had appeared
among them as among the Jewish Christians.
That was God's verdict; and so, in spite of the
extremists, they stretched out to him the hand of
brotherhood and, within certain limits, recognized
his work.[3]

Within certain limits. The most that was
attained was an agreement to differ. The union
meant at the same time separation; Paul was to
go to the Gentiles, Peter to the Jews. Paul
promised besides to collect for the poor at Jerusalem. Probably that helped to dispose the

[1] Gal. 2[2].   [2] Gal. 1[16-18].   [3] Gal. 2[7] sqq.

apostles in his favour. It does not appear to have been an actual condition : he denies in fact that any conditions at all were laid on him.[1]

A recognition of Paul by the authorities—and yet how far from a real solution ! We may learn that from the second scene, a momentary picture, which exhibits Paul in conflict with Peter.[2] Peter paid a visit to Antioch, and showed himself at first very broad-minded ; he did not shrink from sitting at table with the Gentiles. But James, who quite consistently disapproved of his conduct, sent messengers to influence him,[3] and then his vacillating character swung back again. Paul was forced to see others, including even his old colleague Barnabas, led astray, and Peter himself exercising pressure on the Gentile Christians. This provoked him sorely, and here, on his own ground, he dealt out some very plain speaking to the pillar from Jerusalem. The end was a very serious breach of relations. Paul soon departed for a more distant field, and without Barnabas. It is plain that the Jerusalem agreement did not suffice to prevent a very sharp

[1] Gal. 2[6-10].　　[2] Gal. 2[11] sqq.　　[3] Gal. 2[12].

conflict, so soon as Jewish and Gentile Christians really came into contact.

Here the actual thread of events is, for us, broken off short. But the most important feature of the subsequent period is sufficiently clear : Jewish Christianity organized in Paul's own communities an express counter-mission. There are signs that the movement was not confined to Galatia and Corinth.[1]

The agitators obtained, at least for a time, somewhat dangerous successes. They had however at their disposal against Paul effective weapons. Had not Jesus himself lived within the Law ? Had he not been circumcised ? Were not the original apostles the men to decide these things, because they had lived with Jesus ? Was Paul a real apostle ? This question was very seriously pressed.[2] His vision was called an illusion, his authority a usurpation. From their own standpoint these people were not wrong. This question of personal relation to Jesus touched Paul on a vulnerable spot.

The threads of this agitation had their meeting-

[1] Cf. e.g., Phil. 3² sq.
[2] Gal. 1¹, 1² sqq.   II Cor. 10⁷ sqq. ;   11⁶ sqq. ;   12¹¹ sq.

place, no doubt, in Jerusalem. But it remains obscure how the original apostles themselves stood with regard to them. It is not possible to identify them directly with the movement;[1] but without a certain amount of countenance in these circles the emissaries would have had but little prospect of success.[2] The chief suspicion falls on James.

In this memorable strife Paul remains a victor. It is true that he was the representative of progress and natural development, but it is also true that he fought valiantly. He does not seem, however, to have come off without an occasional compromise.

The last time he came to Palestine he had, with regard to Jewish feeling, taken upon himself a true Jewish vow. Out of a similar consideration he had at an earlier time had Timothy circumcised. These notices in the Acts of the Apostles[3] have certainly been keenly contested by criticism; but this criticism rests on the presumption that

[1] The ' apostles beyond measure ' of II Cor. 11^5 and 12^{11} are not the original apostles.
[2] The ' commendatory letters ' of II Cor. 3^1 may refer to this.
[3] Acts 21^{23-26}; 16^3.

Paul behaved with perfect and consistent fidelity to principle. We might perhaps with better right attribute to these accounts, which in spite of an admixture of inaccuracies do not look like pure invention, an exaggerated conception of his consistency. He himself declares that he became ' to those under the law as one under the law.'[1] In either case, he at least did not see in this any abnegation of his cause ; and from an historical point of view any such accommodation is a subordinate matter, for to Paul it was only a means towards the attainment of his fixed end.

Another question necessarily occurs to us : how was it that the controversy did not lead to an absolute cleavage ? Paul would certainly have been revolutionary enough to cut his church clean off from Jerusalem. He was prevented by various causes, but chiefly by the deep-rooted authority of the mother community. It extended far into his own societies ; and Paul himself, even if half against his will, concedes a special high-standing to ' the saints of Jerusalem.' Sharp and pointed remarks, uttered in the heat of

[1] I Cor. 9^{20}.

polemic,[1] must not be allowed to deceive us. Paul was himself a Jewish Christian, conceded to God's people a special claim to salvation, and was able to regard the faith of Gentile Christians as a gift granted them by the real possessors, the believing Jews, a gift which laid them under peculiar obligations.[2] It followed that relations with Jerusalem meant very much to him. The best proof is the importance which he attached to the collection for the poor in that place. This was more than anything else a stroke of ecclesiastical polity ; he desired by this means to improve the feeling towards him in Jerusalem.[3]

[1] e.g., Gal. 2[6].   [2] Rom. 15[27].   II Cor. 8[14].
[3] Rom. 15[31] sq.

III

HIS THEOLOGY

1—Paul as a Theologian

WHEN we call Paul a theologian we must expressly exclude modern associations of the word. He possessed no theological learning in our sense, and has very little affinity with our dogmatic and ethical writers. He never attempts—not even in the letter to the Romans—to unfold a system of doctrine. He writes always as a missionary, an organizer, a speaker to the people, is guided in the setting forth of his thoughts by the occasion given, and treats only of particular sides of his subject. We might well doubt, therefore, whether 'theology' is here the right word to use : but it cannot be avoided.

Two things at least are clear. The first is that in Paul's reasoning a strong theological element

can be discerned, and this is most marked and
distinct when he writes polemically. The influence of his rabbinical schooling comes clearly
into view, both in the style of argument and in
the employment of scripture.[1] The second is
that Paul himself tells us clearly enough what
his estimate of knowledge (gnosis) is. He declares
that he preaches to mature Christians not merely
the simple gospel but also what he calls ' wisdom.'[2]
It is, so to say, a science of the inspired, something
quite different from human wisdom, and quite
unintelligible to the ' natural man.' It is the
' spirit,' he holds, which imparts this wisdom ;
for the spirit knows those things which are above
the intellect, and reveals them. We should call it
theosophy, or visionary religion. It is concerned
with the understanding of mysterious scripture
sayings, and especially with an insight into the
ways and purposes of God, and a foreknowledge
of future developments.[3]

True, all this lay at the circumference rather
than at the centre. If this were all, the theological
element could easily be subtracted from Paul's

[1] Examples : Gal. 3 and 4 ; II Cor. 3.   [2] I Cor. 2⁶·¹⁶.
[3] Example : Rom. 9–11.

religion. But this is by no means all. The total theory of things which is put forward in the apostle's writings includes a wealth of theological hypotheses, propositions, and inferences ; Christianity as a whole appears, to a certain degree, as a structure of thought.

What then is the relation between this and Paul's religion ? The answer is, the two cannot be separated. *The religion of the apostle is theological through and through : his theology is his religion.* The idea that we can find in him a cold doctrine, to be grasped by the understanding, a doctrine which soars more or less beyond the reach of mere piety, is false ; and equally false is the idea that the piety of Paul can be described without mention of those *thoughts* in which he had apprehended Christ, his death and his resurrection. In the very moment of his conversion it was a clear, formulable thought that stamped the new impress upon his life. The single sentence, ' Jesus is Messiah,' with its immediate implications —this was all : but this is the germ of a dogma, and Paul's ' theology ' is only the evolution of the germ.

* * * * * * * *

Let us consider Paul the theologian somewhat closer.

It is easy to see that his ways of thought are somewhat elastic. Certain main lines remain unalterable; for the rest, the thought wavers and alters with heedless freedom from one letter to another, even from chapter to chapter, without the slightest regard for logical consistency in details. His points of view and leading premisses change and traverse each other without his perceiving it. It is no great feat to unearth contradictions, even among his leading thoughts. Here we read : the Gentiles have also a law in their conscience, by which they can be guided ; and soon afterwards : from Adam to Moses sin cannot be imputed to mankind, for there was then no law.[1] When the second thought occurred to Paul, he had clearly forgotten the first. Or again, by the side of the thought that man is not justified by works, but by faith, we find the other thought that in the judgment men will be dealt with according to their works. Tortured attempts to reconcile these opposites are in all such cases

[1] Rom. 2[14] sqq. and 5[13].

mischievous. It is also dangerous, however, to
hold that Paul could not have meant a thing,
because it leads to impossible consequences.
The consequences may be 'impossible,' but did
Paul perceive them? We may perhaps find
instruction in the very fact that he did not.

This fragmentary style of thinking is partly a
result of the rabbinical schooling. Among the
rabbis all discussions start from isolated scripture
texts, or particular problems. The thought moves
from case to case, without any feeling for the
systematic connexion of the whole.

It is better known how much the Pauline method
of scripture proof owes to the rabbis. Paul was
of course very far from having any historical
conception of the Old Testament. He shared
with his age a belief in its verbal inspiration.
In spite of all his attacks on the Law he never
felt any doubt concerning the book of the divine
revelation, and proof from scripture is important
to him, not merely to confute Jewish opponents,
but for its own sake. As a matter of fact, indeed,
he .generally extracts from scripture only that
which he has himself read into it. A favourite
device of his is the method of allegorical interpre-

tation, by which we escape from the yoke of
the letter, without derogating from its sanctity.
Here the motto is, ' Anything can mean anything,'
if only one recognizes the secret sense. Arbitrari-
ness is exalted into a principle ; but still, there
is method in it. When, for instance, Paul quotes
' Thou shalt not muzzle the ox that treadeth
out the corn ' in order to ask ' Does God care for
oxen ? or are not his words intended altogether
for us ? '[1] he is proceeding on the principle that
scripture can say nothing that is not worthy of
God. And when he instructs the Greeks of
Galatia that the promise to ' the seed of Abraham '
can only refer to Christ, because ' the seed,'
and not ' the seeds,' is spoken of, he is making
use of a rule of exegesis which was frequently
followed.[2]

The employment of scripture, however, as a
book of oracles is, from a theological point of
view, more important. In this practice again
Paul stands upon the shoulders of his teachers ;
but he, and indeed the Christians generally,
made a very considerable advance in it. The

[1] I Cor. 9[9] sq.   [2] Gal. 3[16].

tendency to find oracles in the Old Testament grew enormously, and everything now referred, as their views necessitated, to Jesus and the end of the world. The principle behind all this is, 'whatever was written was written for our sake.'[1] The Old Testament is turned by such treatment more and more into a Christian book.

Strange as these things seem to a modern man, there is much in the apostle's actual structure of thought that is far more strange. Much appears to him clear as day, which is by no means clear to us, even to those who especially appeal to his authority. He possessed, we may say, a logic of his own, which differs essentially from ours.

Paul is capable of understanding by the phrase 'the head of the man' his own head, and, in the same breath, Jesus Christ. He justifies the custom of uncovering the head during divine service by the argument that they who do otherwise put to shame their head—that is, Christ. For us this is a mere play upon words. Paul is quite insensitive to the change of meaning. He allegorizes, so to speak, his own thoughts, and

---

[1] e.g., Rom. 15⁴; I Cor. 10¹¹.

takes the allegorical reference as seriously as he does the actual.[1]

But these strange ways of thinking penetrate even into the fundamental conceptions of the apostle. An example of this will at the same time prepare the way for our presentation of his doctrine.

A great part is played in this theology by the thought that what happens to the first of an historical series happens in consequence to the whole series. Adam is the headspring of humanity. He represents the whole race of mankind. What is true of him is therefore true of all that are connected with him. Since he dies, all who belong to his race also die. Christ is again the first of a series. Therefore, since he arises from the dead, all rise with him—simply on that account.[2] In one place Paul formulates the law quite definitely : ' As the earthly (Adam) is, so are they that are earthly, and as the heavenly (Christ) is, so are they that are heavenly.'[3]

---

[1] I Cor. 11[2] sqq. A similar case occurs in I Cor. 10[16] sq., where ' the body of Christ ' is at once the actual body and the community.

[2] Rom. 5[12] sqq. ; I Cor. 15[22] ; and other places.

[3] I Cor. 15[48].

Similarly Abraham is conceived as the type of
all those who are his true sons, that is, who
believe as he did. What then may be observed
in him can, as a matter of course, be predicated
also of them.[1]

We for our part can see no reason whatever
for such deductions from the leader of a line
to those that follow him. We ask at once for a
connexion to be established. Why and how has
the experience of Adam or of Christ such an
effect on other men ? For Paul, on the other
hand, the matter is one of immediate evidence.
He assumes an undefinable coherence between
the race and the individual,[2] and he sees in their
history a parallelism which simply could not but
be so. In other words, he thinks under a law
which does not obtain for us.

In general terms, nothing is more aloof from
Paul's thinking than rational deduction, such as
a religious thinker strives after to-day. This
can be recognized especially in his treatment
of history. Everywhere he sees divine purposes

[1] Gal. 3⁶ sqq.

[2] This is most clear in the case of Christ, because here all
ideas of heredity are excluded.

in the course of things. That is natural and
almost inevitable when history is the object of
religious thought. But he sees in history no slow,
gradual, rationally ascending evolution ; rather
it proceeds by hard oppositions and cleavages ;
for God's ways are by no means even and clear ;
it is incidental to their very nature that they
should be paradoxical and should confound
the wit of man. The Law, according to Paul,
had no preparative, educational significance ; it
did not bring mankind nearer to salvation, not
even by awakening the yearning for redemption.
Rather it resembled—the comparison refers to
ancient customs—those slaves who as guardians
and ' trainers ' have the direction of lads
before they come of age, and deprive them of
their freedom. It only enthralled, and reduced
to misery, for it called sin into being.[1] It was
right that it should be so, says Paul ; God willed
it so—the thought is not too hard for him. But
God had even then the secret purpose to set aside
this dispensation of destruction ; and his grace
should by dint of this contrast shine forth with

---

[1] Gal. 3²⁴ ; 4¹ sq. ; 3¹⁹ ; Rom. 5²⁰.

all the greater brilliance. It is true that this final aim of God hovers, as a last thought, over all, even over the hardening of the people of Israel, which God also willed.[1] All that is harsh, discordant, and hard resolves itself at last in the harmonious exultation of the redeemed.

These are but aspects and specimens of Pauline thinking, not more. The presentation of his theology necessarily affords opportunity to emphasize some other sides of it.

＊ ＊ ＊ ＊ ＊ ＊ ＊ ＊

2—Exposition of Paul's Doctrine

The Pauline world of thought stands in unmistakable contrast to Judaism. But this antagonism governs no more than a definite circle of ideas. Paul's actual doctrine of redemption is not among them ; it is a complete whole in itself. It seems well to describe first of all this separate whole, the doctrine of redemption, and then what is opposed to Judaism. It must not however be supposed that these two things, which we separate for the sake of convenience,

[1] Rom. 9 ; 11³³.

are really two entirely separate and distinct entities, or were so regarded by Paul. The two bodies of thought are, in truth, continuously in contact at many points, and both have their centre in Christ.

At this point the reader who desires to follow us is expressly begged to discard, as far as he possibly can, any conceptions he may have formed of Pauline doctrine. Among all the innumerable Christians of the various churches, who believe that they share Paul's views, there is to-day no single one who could be said to understand them in the sense in which they were really meant ; and the same is true of those who regard themselves as opposed to the apostle's teaching. At most a few members of certain small societies approximate to a true understanding of it. But it is harder to interpret Paul's doctrine to one who half understands him than to one who knows nothing about him.

* * * * * * * *

A—Christ and Redemption from the Powers of the Present World

We do not begin with a doctrine of God. The most characteristic utterance of Paul about God is just this, that he sent Christ for the salvation of men. That is to say, the whole Pauline doctrine is a doctrine of Christ and his work ; that is its essence.

These two, the person and the work of Christ, are inseparable. The apostle had not reached a conception of Christ as a detached object of doctrine, which may be considered without reference to his significance for the world. Paul's essential thought of him is simply this, that he is the redeemer. But with this proviso the utterances about Christ may still to a certain extent be detached from the whole. We shall make the attempt, because it helps us better to understand them, and also because Paul's Christology has attained such a remarkable historical importance.

* * * * * * * *

a—The Chief Lines of Paul's Christology

The ordinary conception of a Messiah does not suffice to characterize the Christ of Paul. For the significance of the Pauline Christ is valid, not for Judaism, but for mankind. On the other hand he is, in essence, something quite different from a man raised up to be Messiah.

This essential character is expressed most simply

and clearly in the name ' Son of God.'[1] He is metaphysically conceived : the Son of God is as such a superhuman, a divine figure. There is no mention, indeed, of a divine procreation : but his origin lies nevertheless in God—God is ' the Father of our Lord Jesus Christ '—and he assuredly has his share in the spiritual, insensible nature of the one God ; he is a celestial being. He is older than all created things ; Paul even makes the far-reaching assertion that he took part as agent in the creation of the world: ' through him were all things created.'[2]

A full conception of this wonderful being can, however, only be gained from the history of his experience. At first he was in heaven (*preexistence*), then he lived on earth in the form of a man, then returned into heaven, into his former glory. In this last phase he receives even more than he had once renounced, for he is now endowed with the full power of the divine governance— a reward for the self-humiliation which he endured through obedience to God and love towards men.[3]

---

[1] Other titles are, e.g., ' the heavenly man ' (I Cor. 15^{45} sqq.) ' the image of God.'

[2] I Cor. 8^6 ; Col. 1$^{15.17}$.

[3] Phil. 2$^{6-11}$; cf. Rom. 1^4 and other places.

The two periods of life in heaven offer no difficulty to the understanding. The crucial point lies
in the conception of Christ's humanity.

In taking on manhood Christ resigns his divine
mode of existence ; his manhood is a contradiction
to it, and therein a contradiction to his real,
essential nature. Paul calls it an ' emptying,'
that is of his divinity. In heaven the Son lived
in the ' form of God,' as a man he wears the
' form of a slave.' An ' impoverishment ' has
taken the place of his former ' riches ' ; the
poverty lies in manhood as such, not in any special
lowliness in the life of Jesus. He appeared ' in
the form of sinful flesh,' whereas he had hitherto
been a spiritual being.[1]

These sayings have all a peculiar emotional force.
It is to Paul the miracle of all miracles that the
Son of God could give himself to such abasement.
But above all they show that Paul assuredly lays
stress on a *substantial change* which comes to pass
through the entering upon manhood.   This will
appear even more clearly through something else.

What *we* prize in the man Jesus plays no part

---

[1] Phil. 2⁶ sq. ; II Cor. 8⁹ ; Rom. 8³.

whatever in the thought of the apostle. Nothing is further aloof from him than religious veneration for a hero. The moral majesty of Jesus, his purity and piety, his ministry among his people, his manner as a prophet, the whole concrete ethical-religious content of his earthly life, signifies for Paul's Christology—nothing whatever.[1] The ' manhood ' appears to be a purely formal thing.

This whole conception of the humanity of Christ confuses us, and the question seriously presents itself if it is not a mere appearance. We are tempted to think of those heretical teachers of the ancient church who held that Christ had a body in appearance only, and the crucifixion had not really touched him at all. But Paul would decidedly reject such a view. Very much depends for him on the reality of the humanity of Christ—so much that without it Christ could not be the redeemer of men. And indeed if a man is a being with father and mother, who walks the earth, possesses a body of flesh, is subject to death, then the Pauline Christ is a real man.

---

[1] The ' obedience ' of which Rom. 5[19] speaks is that of the heavenly being, who humbles himself to a life on earth, and even to the cross.

In our view, no doubt, manhood includes more than this. And if a man is a being who possesses human thought, feeling, and will—not merely in a universal sense, but in his own definite, individual way—then this Christ is not a real man. The truth is, Paul lacks the idea of personality, of human individuality; and therefore the humanity of Christ, as he conceives it, remains for us an impalpable phantom.

It is indeed unthinkable that a being in substance divine should enter into a true union with humanity. Humanity will not accord with his nature. The formulas which Paul uses clearly express so much. He does not say outright, the Son of God became a man, but 'he appeared in the form (or, the image) of man,' he was 'found in appearance as a man,' he came 'in the form of sinful flesh.' Humanity, then, is something strange to him, a beggar's garment which the heavenly prince assumes for awhile, to lay aside again.

The question occurs, how, during Christ's time on earth, the divine element in him is related to his humanity. He still remains in a certain sense the person he was; he does not become another. Will not that betray itself, in spite of the human cloak ? We purposely refrain from going into this question, in order not to direct attention to non-essential points. The essential point is and remains this, that the earthly life of Christ is the opposite of his divine glory ; it is this humiliation alone which chains the interest of the apostle. With regard to this his thought is clean contrary to that of John, according to whom the heavenly radiance of the Son shines forth continually through the veil of flesh, and the earthly life of Christ becomes a revelation of the glory of God.

One thing is clear throughout : Christ had, within himself, no reason whatever to live through a period in the form of a man, which for him betokens nothing but loss. The reason lies in man alone. For his salvation—we anticipate so far—depends entirely on the death and the resurrection of Christ. For this reason, and for no other, there was need that Christ should become a man. In effect, the Son of God becomes a man in order to die and to rise again. Hence it becomes clear how this doctrine flows into the doctrine of redemption, and cannot be understood without it.

* * * * * * * *

b—The Doctrine of Redemption

Three questions arise of themselves : (1) Wherein lies the misery from which the redemption releases us ? (2) How and by what means does Christ bring the redemption to pass ? (3) In what does the benefit of this redemption consist ?

(1) The Misery of Mankind before Christ and without Christ

The redemption is, according to Paul, in a phrase which is brief and yet exact, release from the misery of this whole present world.[1] Every other conception of it, even release from sin, would be too narrow. The character of this present world is determined by the fact that men are here under the domination of dark and evil powers. The chief of these are the ' flesh,' sin, the Law, and death.

To Paul these are not mere abstract terms as they are to us. Thinking, as he did, in the modes of the ancient world he regarded such abstractions as effective powers, almost as actual

[1] Gal. 1⁴.

beings.[1] Sin appears, so to put it, as an active
agent ;[2] death stands in the same rank with
superterrestrial spirits, whom Christ overcomes,
and is destroyed by him like an individual
being.[3]

All these powers stand in the closest alliance.
He that is delivered up to the one falls a victim
to the others also. The most important relation
is that between the flesh and sin.

The word *flesh*—though it often has a more
general meaning—signifies in the most characteristic usage of Paul the external, material
part of man, his bodily self. Every man ' is
in the flesh,' that is, he stands in a finite, sensuous
existence. But this, of itself, implies sin. Sin
clings indissolubly to the flesh, ' dwells ' in the
flesh, originates indeed in the flesh and its impulses.
The phrase ' flesh of sin ' is alone enough to express
this.[4] It is true that Paul, in another treatment

---

[1] Let the reader reflect how ' Love ' (Eros, Amor) was
deified by the ancients, or how among the so-called Gnostics
' the Word,' ' Wisdom,' ' Life,' etc., issue as beings out of
the primal cause of things. This is simply a heightened form
of what we discern in Paul.

[2] Rom. 7[8] sqq.   [3] I Cor. 15[26].

[4] Rom. 7[13] sqq. esp. vv. [14], [18], [20], [23] (members = flesh) ;
8[3] ; 6[6] (body of sin).

of the matter, of a more historical kind, derives sin from the sin of Adam[1]—not however in the later ecclesiastical sense. But if we throw out the question (which he does not himself put) whence came the sin of Adam, hardly any other reply would be possible than to point once more to the flesh.

Man then, through his mere earthly and bodily existence, is made subject to the power of sin. Sin is not merely to be found, as a matter of fact, in all men, but is a necessity.

To embitter this servitude yet more the Law comes into play. The Law turns sin into a punishable transgression, into guilt ; it even increases sin, by stimulating it in order to exercise its own power ; and if it gives man a ' knowledge of sin,' that only means, it makes him aware how forlorn is his state.[2] What, however, reveals his misery most clearly is that sin, implacably and by a firmly rooted law, draws death in its train, a death after which there is no life more. What remains then at last to man ? Nothing but the cry—in which the word ' body ' must not

---

[1] Rom. 5[12] sqq.
[2] Rom. 4[15] ; 7[7] sqq. [18] ; 5[20] ; Gal. 3[19] ; Rom. 3[20].

be overlooked—' Unhappy man that I am, who will rescue me from this body of death ? '[1]

The state of unredeemed humanity is thus, then, in fact, completely depicted. But the picture is supplemented by a view taken from a particular standpoint. Paul believes that mankind without Christ is under the sway of mighty spirits, demons, and angelic powers.

Angels, in our time, belong to children and to poets ; to Paul and his age they were a real and serious quantity. But he does not by any means see in them only friendly helpers and servants of God. A great part of these beings are set upon their own independent dominion, and stand in hostile rivalry to God. These are the ' powers,' ' forces,' ' dominions,' ' heights ' to which his letters often refer.[2] In Paul's mind they tend to be confused with those ' demons '— originally distinguished from them—at whose head Satan stands.

The government, then, of ' this ' world is really controlled by these beings ; God has for a time

[1] Rom. 7[24].
[2] I Cor. 15[24] ; Col. 1[16] ; 2[10, 15]. (Also ' the elements of the world,' Gal 4[3, 9] ; Col. 2[8, 20], are angelic powers).

resigned it to them. The names given above imply as much, and, more clearly still, the title ' Rulers of this world.'[1] Men are given up to the malice and the power of this spiritual realm. If neither ' angels nor powers ' are able to separate the redeemed from the love of God,[2] before redemption they clearly possessed this power ; man lay under their sway.

The whole conception of the misery of mankind is in this way transferred, so to speak, into the supersensual region. Or it all goes on at the same time in two spheres, above and below. For indeed the dominion of the demons cannot be separated from the dominion of sin and its allies. It is the demons who allure and tempt man to sin, especially to the sin of idolatry ;[3] it is the devil who brings about the death of the flesh ;[4] and even behind the Law the angels stand, for they communicated it to Moses, and are its patrons.[5]

The state of mankind could not be more forlorn. No star shines upon this darkness. And the condition of the individual makes no difference in it. Be he better or worse, pious or impious,

[1] I Cor. 2[6], [8].   [2] Rom. 8[38].   [3] I Cor. 10[20].
[4] I Cor. 5[5].   [5] Gal. 3[19] sq., cf. Heb. 2[2] ; Acts 7[38], [51].

it is all beside the question—he remains lost.
Even the Jew has no advantage.

There can, then, while this is so, be no redemption. Man must go forth from this fleshly, earthly
existence into a spiritual, immaterial existence, out
of the sphere of sin into that of righteousness,
out of the reach of the Law into the region of
freedom, out of death into eternal life, out of
the dominion of spirits into the dominion of God.
However central the thought of sin is, in Paul's
mind, still—we reiterate—redemption is *more* than
liberation from sin. Man must be freed from the
bonds of the body and the earthly world, that is,
he must die. Die and become ! So runs the motto.

And he who achieves this liberation is Christ.

(2) The Death and Resurrection of Christ as the Means of Redemption

Two experiences of one single being bring in the
change for all mankind. How is that possible ?
It is intelligible only when we know what death
and resurrection mean for Christ himself.

This meaning rests altogether on the fact that
he becomes a man. For this again means nothing
else but that he enters into that state of human

H

misery which has just been described. He
assumes flesh, and the flesh is in his case also,
as Paul expressly says,[1] the flesh of sin. He
enters therefore into relation with sin, gives
himself into its power. ' Him who [in his heavenly
existence] knew not sin did God for us make [in
his becoming a man] into sin.'[2] This thought,
indeed, is not easy to apprehend. Of course Paul
does not mean that Christ committed sin ; that
is out of the question. But he is thinking of a
general, so to speak an objective sinfulness,
incidental to human nature, as it exists before it
reaches the point of actual transgression. As a
man Christ comes also under the power of the Law,
and, since he wears the flesh of sin, it threatens
him like all sinners with its curse.[3] Lastly his
assumption of humanity brings him into the
dominion of the spirits. For it was these spirits
who really crucified him.[4]

[1] Rom. 8³.   [2] II Cor. 5²¹.   [3] Gal. 4⁴ ; cf. 3¹⁰, 1³.
[4] I Cor. 2⁶⁻⁸. The verses are not applicable to Pilate
and such as he. Paul means, the demons have fallen into
their own pit. They thought to destroy Christ by the
crucifixion. They would not have crucified him if they had
known the wisdom of God, if, that is, they had suspected that
the cross of Christ would bring salvation to the world, and
make an end of them.

As a consequence of all this the necessity of his death becomes clear. He must die because he is a man ; for he has taken upon himself that which, in the case of all men, leads to death, especially sin.

But at this point the thought turns suddenly and completely about. Death is at the same time the liberation of Christ from all these powers of perdition. Through death he passes again utterly out of their sphere ; he no longer wears flesh, and therefore has nothing more in common with sin, law, and death. ' He died,' we read, ' to sin once for all,' and ' death is no more lord over him.'[1] To express it otherwise : the powers into whose dominion he entered make him feel their might upon the cross, but in the same moment they inflict loss upon themselves, are overpowered by him, and through his resurrection he enters upon a new existence, which is not subject to them.

Let us remind ourselves at this point that Paul regards Christ as the representative of the human race.[2] Our question then receives the simple

---

[1] Rom. 6^{10}, ^{9}.   [2] See above, pp. 81 sq.

answer—what happened to Christ, happened to
all. From the moment of his death all men are
redeemed, as fully as he himself, from the hostile
powers, and together with his resurrection all
are transferred into indestructible life. ' One
died for all ; therefore all died.' ' God sent his
son in the form of the flesh of sin and condemned
[to death, in his death] the sin in the flesh ' ;
that is to say, with the destruction of his flesh
the whole sum total, so to speak, of flesh, and
the sin that clings to it, are put away. ' Christ
has redeemed us from the curse of the Law, in
that he became a curse for us ' ; that is to say,
being as a man subject to the Law he fell of
necessity under its curse, but lifted this curse
from all men when by his death he escaped
from the sphere of the Law. Again, the death
on the cross is a triumph over the angelic powers ;
they are brought thereby into derision.[1]

The death of Christ, then, has certainly a
vicarious significance, but not in the sense of the
doctrine of the church ; if only for this reason,
that the resurrection is equally vicarious.[2]

[1] II Cor. 5[14] ; Rom. 8[3] ; Gal. 3[13] (4[4]) ; Col. 2[15].
[2] II Cor. 5[15], ' dead and raised again for us.'

Moreover in this view of it the relation of Christ's resurrection to his death is quite especially simple. It is not merely the divine Amen to the death of the son of God, not merely its legitimation; it is in a truer sense the reverse side of that death itself. Death is the laying aside of the old garment, resurrection is the assumption of the new. The one does not exist apart from the other. The question which Paul regarded as the more important is void of meaning.

It must be owned that speculation concerning the death of Christ is, in Paul, much more richly developed than concerning the resurrection. This view of the death which we have expounded, a view which is put forward in the most diverse letters of Paul, is not the only view which he knows ; only, as appears to us, the most definite and complete. It is not without reason that more thoughts gather about the death. The resurrection requires no interpreter, it simply *is* the entrance into the glorious life. On the other hand, the death on the cross receives its content, its significance, only through interpretation of its meaning ; in itself it has nothing to do with redemption. And, besides this, the death of

Christ was naturally a difficult problem to Paul, a problem which attracted his thought.

(3) The Benefit of the Redemption

The state of the redeemed is described by Paul quite consistently in accordance with the doctrine already unfolded. He says that they ' are dead ' or ' are risen again ' ' with Christ ' ; or more specifically ' they are dead to sin, to the Law,'[1] ' crucified to the world ' ; ' the body of sin is destroyed ' ; ' they are no longer in the flesh ' ; or else he says simply that they are ' dead.'[2] The collective force of these utterances is that they have left behind them this whole present world.

The danger of misunderstanding is perhaps nowhere so great as at this point. All such utterances are traditionally apprehended in an *ethical* sense. The death here spoken of is taken to be a figure, derived from the death of Christ, and signifying the successful struggle against sin ; though the extraordinary fondness of the apostle

[1] The same phrase is used of the believers (Rom. 6[2]) as of Christ (Rom. 6[10]).

[2] Rom. 6[4], [8]; Col. 3[1] ; Rom. 6[2],[11], 7[4] ; Gal. 2[19], 6[14] ; Rom. 6[6], 8[9] ; Col. 3[3], and other places.

for this figure remains unexplained. But in truth these expressions are intended *actually and literally*. Paul is thinking of a real death, such a death as Christ has undergone, a participation in his death. The liberation from sin is the consequence of this death, and is therefore implied in it ; but it is only a part of the whole, if a very important part. This literal acceptance of these expressions is demanded by the consistency of the whole doctrine. If the misery of man consists in his habitation in the flesh, his happiness must depend on his liberation from the flesh, that is, on his death.

The misinterpretation referred to is nevertheless very natural. For the believer still wears the body of flesh, and is still in the world ; the life of glory has not yet begun. And Paul himself, of course, is continually saying so. He says the same, indeed, even of sin. Their power, according to his doctrine, is broken ; and yet every one of his exhortations presupposes that their power is not yet broken.

Here, then, on the face of things, is a contradiction. The redemption is said to be perfect, and yet it is not perfect, because the fleshly

body has not yet been laid aside. In the mean-
time 'your life is [still] hidden with Christ in
God.'[1] But Paul is certainly not aware of any
contradiction, for he gives utterance to both,
the 'already' and the 'not yet,' in the same
breath; he is especially partial to the form :
you are dead to sin; therefore let it have no more
dominion in you.[2]

We might say, Paul's words on the redemption
anticipate what the future is to bring. But for
the apostle the redemption is already a perfect
truth, because Christ *has already* died and risen
again. Since all is now prepared, it is as good
as if it had begun. The death and resurrection
of Christ include the death and resurrection of
all. The former are accomplished, unalterable
facts—so then are the latter also. But still the
outward realization of that which, in the ideal
sense, has already happened is reserved for the
future.[3]

---

[1] Col. 3[8].   [2] e.g., Rom. 6[8-18].

[3] The wording of Gal. 2[20] is characteristic : ' I have been
crucified with Christ ; that which lives is no more I, but
rather Christ lives in me. *But the life which I now live in the
flesh* I live in faith on the Son of God.' The life in the flesh
is only, as it were, a remainder.

This is very important. The whole Pauline conception of salvation is characterized by suspense ; a suspense which strains forwards towards the final release, the actual death. The earthly life is not the setting in which salvation becomes complete.

In this connexion we should keep before our minds with especial clearness a fact which, indeed, when we are dealing with Paul, ought never to be forgotten. He believed with all his might in the speedy coming of Christ and the approaching end of the world. In consequence, the redemptive act of Christ, which lay in the past, and the dawn of the future glory lay, in his view, close together. The redemptive act must itself be reckoned as belonging to the final age ; it is the first act of the last development, an act which must be followed swiftly and of necessity by all the rest. This makes the suspense, the forward outlook, especially intelligible.

It has been popularly held that Paul departed from the view of salvation which was entertained by the oldest community, by shifting the stress from the future to the past, looking upon the blessedness of the Christian as already attained, and emphasizing faith instead of hope. It is easy to see that this is assuredly but a half truth. All references to the redemption as a completed transaction swing round at once into utterances about the future. Certainly, Christ has died and the faithful have died with him, but any elucidation of that thought must show that it loses its meaning if the continuation of what has happened is left out of account. Faith itself is always hope, for what is, is not yet what must be. Out of the innumerable vouchers for this let us take but one. The redeemed are ' sons[1] of God.' In its full sense this expression denotes for the Christian what it denoted for Christ, but derivatively. Those are sons of God who share in the spiritual nature of God, free from the bodily and material, such as ' Christ, the first-born among many brethren,'[2] has possessed since the resurrection. The text runs, you are already sons, no longer slaves—that is, rightly and fundamentally sons ; but goes on immediately, ' we sigh in

---

[1] Paul does not shrink from this expression as the later John does, who says only ' children ' of God. ' Son ' is used by John only of Christ.

[2] Rom. 8²⁹. The ' image of Christ ' = his heavenly state.

expectation of the sonship, namely, the redemption of our body.'[1]

Are we then to say that though the sure foundation of salvation had been laid in the work of Christ, yet its whole realization was deferred ? Not without modification. Something real is already here—the spirit of God.

In Paul's mind this is an extraordinarily important element. He understands by it a supernatural force which enters into man, ' dwells,' works, and acts within him, ' drives ' him.[2] Sometimes he seems even to see in it a heavenly substance, which brings about a substantial change in man. The believer is ' in the spirit,' just as he once was ' in the flesh.'[3] What helps to explain this is that the whole life beyond bears the character of ' the spiritual.' The spirit is ' the spirit of the [superterrestrial] life.'[4] Its possession therefore denotes that a foretaste of

---

[1] Cf. Rom. 8[14] sqq. with 8[23]. Again, the spirits are already overcome through the cross (Col. 2[15]) and must yet in the last time be fought and conquered by Christ (I Cor. 15[24] sqq.).

[2] e.g., I Cor. 3[16] ; Rom. 8[14].

[3] Rom. 8[9]. The indwelling of the spirit of Christ in the body of man gives assurance of resurrection : Rom. 8[11].

[4] Rom. 8[2].

the future life is already here. It is a gift of the last time, in which the forces of that world are already working their way into this existence. Its descent upon mankind is bound up with the resurrection of Christ, through which indeed Christ himself has once more become spirit. Paul assumes that every Christian, in becoming a believer, at once possesses the spirit, and becomes through it a 'son of God.'[1] This is perfectly logical and consistent. Could it be that one who had suffered death with Christ—as every Christian had done—should yet possess no share in his life ? But the spirit becomes plain and manifest in its workings. Its sway shows itself in the miraculous powers and gifts which are daily to be seen in the life of the communities : in the power to heal the sick, in prophecy which surprises the secrets of the future, in the speaking with tongues, where it is visibly not the man himself, but another being, working through him, that speaks, sighs, and cries ' Abba, Father.'[2]   But it is significant that Paul does not think only of supernatural workings such as these. If sin belongs to the nature of

[1] Rom. 8[14] sqq.
[2] I Cor. 12[9] sq. ; Rom. 8[15], [26] ; Gal. 4[6].

this world, the spirit will manifest itself in all that makes against sin, in every good and moral work, in peace, joy, and the assurance of faith ; for all this is unattainable by the natural man.[1]

The apostle here approaches the modern conception that the holy spirit, as a moral force, engenders that which is good in the heart of man. But his view is not identical with this. He does not think of the spirit as penetrating the inmost personality, and becoming one with it. This psychological conception of the matter is strange to him. The spirit always retains the character of a supernatural element, whose sway within the earthly man is that of a foreign power.

For the rest, the very fact that the spirit is already working points once more to the future. The spirit is after all only the ' earnest ' of full salvation, only the ' first-fruits '—the perfect harvest is yet to come.[2]

(4) Review of the Doctrine of Redemption

The structure of this doctrine is very close and compact. Perhaps it may seem to the reader

---

[1] Gal. 5[22] ; I Thess. 1[5].   [2] II Cor. 1[22], 5[5] ; Rom. 8[23].

to be, as a whole, exceedingly complicated ; but
only because this world of ideas is half or altogether
strange to him.   Intrinsically it is very simple,
and a test of this is that it can be expressed in
quite short sentences. Christ, the son of God,
resigns his sonship and becomes a miserable man
like us, that we men may become sons of God ;
Christ enters into the dominion of sin, but overcomes it by his death ; and so we, who languished
in the bonds of sin, are freed from it—such
sentences as these comprise all that the doctrine
imports. They are always a mere variation of the
one theme : Christ becomes what we are, that
we through his death may become what he is.

But certain elucidations are none the less
necessary.

1. The whole picture of the redemption has
something impersonal and cold about it.   Its
accomplishment lies quite outside the individual
man, and its incidents play themselves out,
so to speak, on Christ alone. And yet these
thoughts beget in Paul a warmth of feeling ; to
him they are the expression of the infinite grace
of God. It is the personal love of God that set
all this in train, the self-denying love of Christ

that carries it through. And it is this love that speaks to the heart of the apostle, and gains a response, not from his understanding, but from his feeling, his piety. His theology is to him, in reality, religion.

Many different shades of religious feeling could be named, which form the reflex of this doctrine. But it is characteristic that Paul's mood oscillates between two poles—triumphant joy and expectant longing. This must needs be, because salvation is at once present and future. On the whole the joy preponderates, joy over what God has already wrought. This it is that the apostle has experienced ; this it is wherein he sees the foundation, firm as a rock, for all the rest. But still the longing, which cannot find satisfaction in this, must ever and again break through.[1]

There are deep-reaching differences between the Pauline doctrine of the redemption and the thoughts of modern belief.

2. In the first place, the modern view is apt to transfer the scene of salvation to man himself, or his consciousness. Peace of heart, a pure

[1] Rom. 8²³ sqq. ; II Cor. 5⁸ ; Phil. 1²¹ sqq.

conscience, a confident assurance of grace, a
consciousness of forgiveness—such is the 'present
bliss' of which men speak. Even though eternal
life may exalt it by the removal of earthly limits,
yet the essential is already here. But in all these
subjective states of consciousness Paul does not
in the least perceive salvation ; rather is it in
its own nature something objective, a change in
the very nature and conditions of existence.—
There is another matter of equal importance.

3. We have several times deprecated a one-
sided ethical interpretation of Pauline doctrine.
Its prevalence derives from the fact that people
do not recognize the remoteness of modern
thought from that of Paul. In our view sin is
altogether a matter of the individual will, if not
necessarily of the conscious will. We are accustomed to draw a strict distinction between the
merely natural and the moral. *Paul knows no
such distinction.* For him, flesh and sin cohere
indissolubly together, even in the case of believers.
And therefore redemption does not bring with it
merely an ethical revolution. It signifies rather
a change in the nature of humanity, and the ethical
change is secondary to this.

4. One question has not yet been put : how does the individual man come into possession of salvation ? The answer is simply, through faith and baptism. Of baptism we must speak further. In the matter of faith it is remarkable that Paul makes no attempt to describe it more closely, and to define the signs by which true and false, normal and defective faith can be distinguished. Faith is simply an obedient[1] acceptance of and assent to the preaching of redemption. The conviction of its truth effects at once that mystic union with Christ by dint of which his death and resurrection are automatically transferred to the believer, so that he also is dead and has risen again. Faith can certainly appear also as trust or hope, but no weight is laid on any such definition.

Here again a very considerable difference from the modern conception comes into view. An objective redemption is indeed not unknown to the dogmatic and popular exposition of to-day ; but in their doctrine of salvation they are always thinking of what happens in the individual man.

---

[1] Paul often speaks of ' obedience of faith.'

I

They ask how the process which imparts the benefit of Christianity goes on, and must necessarily go on, in the individual soul. Since the Reformation this has been a central problem. The nature of faith is defined, its relation to the atonement discussed, the question is raised how goodness grows out of faith, and so on. The doctrine of salvation is therefore in great part a doctrine of human piety and its normal origin, or a religious psychology. This whole chapter is absent from the Pauline teaching. The reason is that in his doctrine he is not thinking of the individual at all, or of the psychological processes of the individual, but always of the race, of humanity as a whole. Death with Christ is a general fact, which comes to pass in all believers alike; not an event transacted in the individual soul, and connected with that soul's special experiences and feelings.

And because it is with the race that Paul is concerned, his mode of thinking is purely historical. All his thoughts about salvation are thoughts about a series of events, in which God and man take part, whose scene is on earth and also in heaven—it proceeds, properly speaking, in both places at the same time. Paul has always before his eyes great periods of human development, and thinks in terms of the temporal distinctions, past, present, and to come. All the leading ideas of his theology bear this historical stamp. Flesh and spirit form an antithesis not only in their nature, but in the periods to which they belong ; so too with sin and righteousness, servitude and sonship ; and Christ stands as the turning-point between an old and a new age. This is one of the most essential features of Paul's type of thought. His very piety receives its character from the salvation history ; the history of salvation is the content of his faith.

* * * * * * * *

c—Particular Important Views of Paul in their connexion with the Doctrine of Redemption

We have appraised, as one side of Paul's religious personality, the aversion from the world which marks his appreciation of life. The description of his doctrine gives us to understand how deeply this view of life is grounded in his whole fashion of thought. One who feels as Paul feels the fatality which chains man to the world of sense, can have no real attachment to the possessions, conditions, and institutions of the worldly life. It is all condemned to destruction, all is merely ' flesh,' and the sooner it vanishes the better.

But we must touch upon some other fields of view on which a specially strong light is thrown by the thoughts on the redemption.

Paul's expectation of the future comprises a whole world of concrete—and in part highly fantastic—conceptions. The great drama of the last time, in which God's foes will be destroyed, with its culmination in the resurrection of the dead and the judgment, comes before the ' life ' which death has no more power to kill. These ideas are immediately connected with the doctrine of redemption, which looks forth to the glory that is to come. Moreover, we can also clearly perceive how the picture of the future corresponds, in remarkable fashion, to the account of the redemption. Great prominence is given to the thought of the resurrection—or in the case of those who live to see the coming of Christ, the transformation which takes its place ; this is the direct result of the resurrection of Christ. But it is not the resurrection of the old body, for ' flesh and blood

cannot inherit the kingdom of God.' The state
of the redeemed requires a radiant, clarified,
' spiritual ' body, such as the risen Christ himself
wears.[1] The future life, indeed, cannot wear any
of the colours of sense. Earthly joys, even in
some purer form, can have no validity in heaven.
All national dreams, such as the Jew cherishes,
are also buried with the world of the flesh. But,
together with the believer, the whole creation
undergoes transfiguration. For creation too sighs
in the bonds of the temporal.[2]

If we disregard the half social, half ethical
regulations for the life of the communities, Paul's
ethic, as regards the content of its demands, does
not exhibit many original features. It is in the
main the Jewish ethic, reduced of course—and
the importance of this point is very great—on
the legal side, and augmented by a few Christian features which are not peculiar to Paul.
Chief among these is the emphasis on love, especially brotherly love, such as the life of the small
community requires. Besides this, certain special
motives to moral conduct are made prominent by

[1] I Cor. 15⁵⁰ sqq., ⁴² sqq.   [2] Rom. 8¹⁹ sqq.

the thought of the approaching judgment and the speedy coming of Christ : there is need of sobriety, watchfulness, and in general a worthy preparedness for the decisive hour.

But we can easily see how this ethic, too, is tributary to the leading thoughts, and receives from them a special significance. The idea that the Christian, by dint of the death and resurrection of Christ, stands in a new life, and the idea of the spirit, which in very truth exhibits the new life upon the earth, give the strife against the old man its sharpest accent ; it is necessary to feel the *obligation* which the possession of the spirit involves ; it is necessary to walk ' after the spirit.'[1] But at the same time these ideas encourage the expectation that the fight is not hopeless. If the sanctification of the body and the warfare against sensuality are especially emphasized, that again is closely connected with the conception

[1] This is the characteristic form in which Paul speaks of the spirit as an ethical quantity. He sets up no standard for the individual, by which it may be recognised whether he has the spirit or not. Rather he takes for granted the presence of the spirit in all—it is a tenet of faith that every one possesses it, like the tenet that every one is dead with Christ—and only demands that they shall live in accordance therewith. Note I Cor. 3[16].

of the flesh. We are not here called upon to
depict Paul's strong personal interest in ethical
questions.

Paul recognizes not merely separate communities, but a *church* as a single whole. The
Christians form a body ; they are members one
of another, and likewise members of Christ ; for
he is the head to which the body belongs.[1] The
believers enter into a mystic communion with
Christ, so that all that he has, experiences, and is,
transfers itself in a mysterious way to them.
They are ' in Christ ' and he is ' in them,' just
as they are ' in the spirit ' and the spirit is ' in
them.' Here we find ourselves in the midst of
well-known thoughts.[2] It is self-evident that
the church is much more to the apostle than a
community in worship or a religious society with
a special constitution ; fundamentally the church
is to him the new humanity itself, which is uplifted,
by its unity with the crucified and risen, out of
the whole remaining mass of mankind.

[1] I Cor. 12$^{13\text{-}27}$, 10^{16} sq.
[2] According to Col. 1^{24} the experience even of the individual
believer can pass over into the whole body of Christ ; the
apostle's own sufferings are sufferings of this body, and, so
to speak, supplement the yet uncompleted sufferings of Christ.

Lastly a word about the sacraments. This is especially the point where we can see that the rude, massive views, even, we must say, the superstition and magic of the popular religion are by no means foreign to Paul. His ideas of the sacred acts of baptism and the Lord's Supper, which moreover are not of his creation, were in no wise purely spiritual or symbolic. He certainly can and does find symbols in them, but it is equally certain that they are to him in their own nature real sacraments, that is acts which are intrinsically operative, without the sensibilities and sentiments of the person coming into account. It is a very significant fact that he is not repelled by the custom of baptizing living Christians as substitutes for the dead, in order to extend to them after death the blessing of baptism, and especially to ensure to them the resurrection ; he even derives an argument for the resurrection from it.[1] Such is also the idea that unworthy eating and drinking at the Lord's Supper brings about, by a purely magical operation, sickness and even death,[2] or that the solemn banning of a sinner will result in his bodily destruction.[3]

[1] I Cor. 15²⁹.   [2] I Cor. 11³⁰ sq.   [3] I Cor. 5⁵.

But these very sacramental views enable him to establish the closest connexion between the sacred acts and his doctrine of redemption. The intrinsic change in a man is brought about by intrinsic processes.

Baptism, the act which visibly announces that a Jew or pagan has come to believe, is according to Paul 'baptism into the death of Christ.'[1] Our way of baptizing makes this phrase simply unintelligible, for the phrase presupposes that the person baptized is immersed. It is however, necessary to know that 'baptism' really means only 'immersion'; 'baptize' means 'immerse.' The disappearance of the candidate in the water can now be understood as a symbol of his death, and his emergence as a symbol of his resurrection. But it is much more than a symbol. Baptism is an 'immersion into Christ'; Christ is thereby 'put on' like a garment ;[2] that means, the believer becomes incorporate with Christ, so that he forms, so to say, one person with him. It is only another expression of this same thought to say that he is 'immersed into the death of Christ.' It betokens that he becomes one with this death, that is, that

[1] Rom. 6³ sq.　　[2] Gal. 3²⁷.

he is now also dead. The 'body of sin' finds its death in the water, and there emerges a being with a new nature.[1] An idea closely akin to this is that baptism imparts the spirit. Baptism it is, then, that actually, in conjunction with belief, in a perfectly real if undefinable way, bestows redemption on the individual, and makes him a member of the body of Christ.

The Lord's Supper is similarly conceived. We are here concerned with 'supernatural food' and 'supernatural drink.'[2] And just as he who partakes of a pagan sacrificial meal enters thereby into communion with the demons, so that they can house in him, so he who in the Lord's Supper consumes the body and blood of Christ is thereby brought into communion with Christ.[3] It is true that there has been unity with Christ ever since baptism, but by the Lord's Supper it is renewed and strengthened.

B—The Controversy with Judaism: Law and Faith; Works and Grace

The best known of Paul's ideas, the so-called doctrine of justification by faith, has not yet been

---

[1] Rom. 6[1] sqq.   [2] I Cor. 10[3] sq.   [3] I Cor. 10[16-21].

mentioned. Our silence in itself implies a judgment. The Reformation has accustomed us to look upon this as the central point of Pauline doctrine ; but it is not so. In fact the whole Pauline religion can be expounded without a word being said about this doctrine, unless it be in the part devoted to the Law. It would be extraordinary if what was intended to be the chief doctrine were referred to only in a minority of the epistles. That is the case with this doctrine : it only appears where Paul is dealing with the strife against Judaism.[1] And this fact indicates the real significance of the doctrine. It is the *polemical doctrine* of Paul, is only made intelligible by the struggle of his life, his controversy with Judaism and Jewish Christianity, and is only intended for this. So far, indeed, it is of high historical importance, and characteristic of the man.

Paul waged this war of theories with the whole artillery of his rabbinical learning. He carries it on, indeed, in the most artificial way ; a Jew would

---

[1] It is developed in detail only in the letters to the Galatians and the Romans. By the side of these cf. also the polemical passage Phil. 3⁶⁻⁹.

have had no trouble in exposing one weak
place after another in his intricate arguments.
But it would be very perverse and unfair to rest
in such an impression. Wrapped up in the
cloak of this extraordinary argumentation there
are truly important meanings. It is these inner
tendencies of his thought that are really material.
But to apprehend them we must first enquire
into the motives and aims of the theory. When
these are clear, a survey of the theory itself
is easy.

*   *   *   *   *   *   *   *

a—Motives and Aims of the Polemical Doctrine

One point seems to be particularly clear. As
a missionary Paul could not endure that Jewish
customs, circumcision and all the rest, should be
made a condition of Christianity for the Gentiles.
But if not, then they could not constitute a necessary note of Christianity even for the Jew. At
most they were the private concern of the individual. The strife about these things, however,
laid upon the apostle the necessity of positively
defining the real condition for entering into
Christianity. We might perhaps have expected

him to set up the antithesis : it is not the Jewish
ceremonial that is necessary, but only the moral
element in the Law.[1] But he did not find in this
the real point of divergence. What made a pagan
into a Christian was not morality, and still less
was it morality that separated the Christian
from the Jew. The real distinctive note was
simply belief in Jesus Christ. Here we have the
source of the formula, *not the Law with its works,
but faith*. This set Paul the task of demonstrating
the superfluity, perhaps harmfulness of the Mosaic
ceremonial, and the necessity and adequacy of
belief in Christ. The negative part of this task
was the chief part.

But Paul does not attack simply the Jewish
institutions ; he attacks the whole Law. In the
fullest sense ' Christ is the end of the Law.'[2] At
first sight this is enigmatical. Why are not the
moral commands excepted ? How can belief in
Christ be opposed to them ? Certainly Paul
never dreams that the *content* of the moral precepts,
such as the ten commandments, is false.[3] But

---

[1] A casual formula of this kind is to be found in I Cor. 7[19].
[2] Rom. 10[4].
[3] e.g. Rom. 7[7], [12], [14]. The law itself is holy, etc.

he denies the right of the Law to *demand* their
fulfilment ; he declares that every ' thou shalt '
is done away. Even this is enigmatical enough.

Paul saw himself confronted by the Jewish
religion. It rejected Christ as redeemer, and yet
claimed to lead to the same goal which was
assured by the redemption, that is to eternal
salvation. The way to it lay in the keeping of
the commandments, in doing. But this way of
salvation was incorporated in the Law ; it was the
sense of the *whole Law* to point man to conduct.
The recognition of this revealed in Paul's mind a
divergence of principle. On the one side—God
alone accomplishes all in sending Jesus Christ ;
on the other—it is the works of the Law which
obtain the reward. Here we have the source of
the formula, *not the works of men, but grace*. This
set Paul the task of exhibiting the Jewish way of
salvation as a way of error, and Judaism itself as
a superseded and false religion ; and the grace
which gave all things with the redeemer as the
compendium of the true religion, which alone
leads to the goal. The positive part of this task
was the chief part. The attack on the Jewish
religion is but a means towards an end, that of

defending and establishing his own view of faith.
It is then the doctrine of redemption which forms
the firm ground for the rejection of the Law.
We have here really a defensive doctrine to guard
that of grace, or—and this is the same thing—
that of the redeemer and the worth of his historic
achievement.

Some slight element of caricature enters into
this conception of the Jewish religion ; for it was
not ignorant of grace ; it even laid stress on grace.
But the prevalent feature of that religion is nevertheless touched when the principle of its piety is
found in performance of tasks or in earning of
rewards.   And it was a perception of the highest
possible kind which seized on *Christianity as a
religion with a peculiar principle of its own*, that is,
as *something entirely new*.

Two purposes, then, come really into play :
(1) the mission must be free from the burden of
Jewish national custom ; (2) the superiority of
the Christian faith in redemption over Judaism
as a whole must be assured.   *The doctrine of
justification is nothing more than the weapon with
which these purposes were to be won.*   But in its
exposition it is impossible to keep the two motives

apart, for they are always intertwining and fusing together.

 *   *   *   *   *   *   *   *

b—Fundamental Lines of the Polemical Doctrine Itself

The fundamental Jewish view which Paul has before him, connects salvation, in a very simple way, with the 'righteousness' of the man. If a man keeps the commandments, God in the judgment declares him to be just, or 'justifies' him. He behaves like a judge, who extends to the accused no special favour, but with simple impartiality, according to an established standard, ascertains the facts of the case and gives his judgment accordingly : this judgment is decisive of the fate of the accused.

This juristic doctrine is denied by Paul. He then first shows that no man attains to the divine standard. Acquittal in the judgment could only be gained by keeping the *whole* Law, and no one keeps it all ; therefore all, without exception, are sinners.[1]

But Paul goes further. It never was God's intention that the Law should lead to salvation.

---

[1] Gal. 3[10] sqq ; Rom. 3[9] sqq. [11].

For ' the letter, that is the Law, slays ' ; experience shows that it has a destructive effect ; it only calls sin into being.[1] At this point we could almost expect the thought that the Law is from the devil. Paul is not able to go so far. But he nevertheless ventures to lay stress on the belief that the Law, though ultimately a divine institution, was communicated to Moses *directly* only by the angels, not by God himself, and to see in this a proof of its utter inferiority.[2] In the history of mankind it is then nothing but an interlude, so willed by the inscrutable God.[3]

This is the refutation of the Jewish position. A comprehension of the positive view which Paul opposes to it depends entirely on the perception that he moulded it in the *form* of the Jewish doctrine.

He says, man is justified through faith ; or, faith is reckoned as righteousness.[4] If we take this literally, the Pauline doctrine does not stand above but below the Jewish. The understanding

---

[1] Gal. 3[21, 19]; II Cor. 3[6].

[2] Gal. 3[19] sq. Verse 20 says that a spokesman is only needed by a plurality of persons (in this case the angels).

[3] Gal. 3[15-25].   [4] e.g. Rom. 4[2] sqq.

K

of the laity—not of the worst men—has felt this thousands of times. It could not be argued out of the conviction that conduct, even though imperfect, must still have more worth than belief, than persuasion, which costs no exertion at all. In the creation of this impression Paul himself is not innocent, and that because he made use of the Jewish scheme. If the religious teaching of children, contrary to all sound pedagogic, labours even to-day with Paul's formulas, the result is fairly certain : faith appears as the one performance which is really pleasing to God—whether the thought is found acceptable by moral laxitude, or is simply cast away by moral energy.

But Paul's real meaning was something else. What he intends to say is truly this, that our relation to God does not depend on performance and merit, not even on that of faith. God justifies man ' freely,' ' of grace.'[1] And ' justify ' in this connexion means nothing more than that he absolves him of his sin, and unconditionally confers upon him his grace, which is then appropriated by faith. That is to say, the expression ' justify '

---

[1] Rom. 3²⁴, cf. also 4⁴.

loses its juristic sense altogether, in fact entirely
excludes juristic ideas from the relation between
man and God ; it is really an unsuitable expression—the best proof that Paul chose it only on
account of the Jewish doctrine. The thought is
therefore, God does not appear before man as
judge at all ; he shows himself rather as giver.
In this way there emerges, out of forms which are
so easily capable of misunderstanding, a description, as simple as it is apt, of the nature of piety.
For the truly religious element in religion, such
as corresponds to the consciousness of every pious
man, is that man stands over against God simply
as the receiver, and God alone is the giver.

This emphasis on grace is the point wherein
Luther really coincides with Paul. Otherwise
Luther's doctrine is by no means conterminous
with this Pauline theory, precisely as the one
repeats the formulas of the other. The very
difference between them may serve to show Paul's
meaning in a clearer light.

Luther asks, how does the individual man,
who stands in the church and shares the church's
faith in the redemption, overcome the tormenting
uncertainty whether salvation and the forgiveness

of sins holds good personally for him ? His
answer is, he reaches a personal certainty when he
recognizes that it depends absolutely on grace,
which God has unconditionally promised. Paul
has not the individual in mind at all ; the question
of personal certainty of salvation therefore plays
no part in his exposition. He asks, as we have
seen, quite generally, what is the condition of
entry into the church ? and finds the answer in
faith ; and again, quite generally, what is the
way by which humanity attains salvation ? and
points to grace, which has been manifested in the
redemption.[1] We must not then conceive justification as a personal experience of the individual,
or a subjective, psychical process. It is rather
conceived in the same mode as the death of Christ,
which holds good for all who belong to Christ.
At bottom justification is nothing else than
Christ's historic act of redemption, namely his
death. By this act God has declared for all men
that grace and faith, not works and law, are
really important.

The question, then, of the meaning of the death

[1] In Luther too ' faith ' has the note of purely personal
trust ; not so in Paul.

of Christ occurs once more. · It cannot be denied that Paul interpreted it by means of sacrificial ideas, especially that of the sin-offering.[1] That does not however in itself prove more than that the effect which, according to Jewish opinion, the blood of the victim possessed, is assigned— without any more detailed analogy coming into consideration—to the blood of Christ. His death is taken to be the death of a sacrifice ; it has therefore the same virtue as the sacrifice, namely the expiation or remission of sins ; that is, it confers righteousness on man.

Nevertheless it is customary to presume in this connexion an elaborate theory of the death of Christ, a theory which is quite or nearly identical with the orthodox doctrine of the church. God could not, because of his justice and holiness, be gracious to sinful men ; he could not but punish them. But Christ, who being sinless himself, need not have died, suffered in their stead the punishment of death. The justice of God was thereby satisfied, and he was able to let his grace prevail.—Undoubtedly much can be said

[1] e.g., Rom. 3^{25} ; I Cor. 5^7.

for such an interpretation of several Pauline sayings.[1] Still, we do not believe in it. First of all, Paul never says that God *could not forgive* until his justice was satisfied. And that would be a most surprising fact : for this assumption always forces itself into prominence wherever this view is cherished. Paul, again, never speaks of a reconciliation *of God* ; it is God's own *love* which, after the time of enmity, *brings about* reconciliation and peace.[2]

It is moreover remarkable that in this connexion the idea appears once more, that all that is true of Christ becomes necessarily true of his members. The obedience of one, it reads, becomes the righteousness of all.[3] This polemical doctrine is always leading back into the old thoughts on the redemption. He who is freed from sin, is simply righteous.[4] And so righteousness may be taken to be the outflow of the new life, which the Christian through his death receives from Christ.

[1] The weightiest instance is Rom. 3[24] sqq., but another interpretation is possible.

[2] Rom. 5[8] sqq.   [3] Rom. 5[18] sq.

[4] Rom. 6[16] sqq. The shade of meaning in ' righteous ' is somewhat different, according as forgiveness of guilt or liberation from the power of sin is spoken of.

It would not indeed be hard to show that this death itself coincides fundamentally with justification.

But, as before, the righteousness which man receives only comes to full reality in the future. The first impression, indeed, is strongly against this idea. Righteousness appears clearly as a benefit already present, which is necessarily followed, but only in the future, by the benefit of eternal life.[1] But Paul only makes this severance because in the Jewish doctrine eternal life was conceived as the consequence of the righteousness gained on earth. In truth righteousness is only present in the sense that the death of Christ, which brings it into being, is an undoubtedly certain fact. But it can equally well be regarded as the object of hope.[2]

Paul himself, like his followers afterwards, was obliged to hear the reproach that his doctrine favoured moral indifference, because it laid all on grace and rejected the Law. He answered that the spirit, of itself, did all that the Law could require.[3]

---

[1] Rom. 5[1] sqq., [9] sq.   [2] Gal. 5[5].
[3] Rom. 6[1], [15] ; Gal. 5[18], [22] sq.

But it cannot be denied that the radical rejection of the Law has something artificial about it. No ethical religion can dispense with the thought that God gives commandments to men. Paul himself bears witness to this ; for in his writings the thought of the Law is continually forcing its way in, whether he speaks of the ' law of Christ ' or of the condensation of the Law in the law of ' love thy neighbour.'[1] What else, indeed, have we before us, when again and again he enforces, in imperatives, the moral commandments ? But even more : when polemic is silent, the law of retribution appears again without disguise : God judges according to works. This doctrine then has not been consistently elaborated.

Still, from an historical point of view, the chief point remains that this doctrine protects Christianity from institutions, and that it expresses the distinction between Christianity and Judaism, and therewith, for the first time, the full consciousness of the unique character of the Christian religion. In this respect chapters 3 and 4 of Galatians are the monument of a memorable moment in the history of religion.

[1] Gal. 6², 5¹⁴ ; Rom. 13⁸ sq.

The release from Judaism is not, however, perfect. Paul himself, in spite of all, never entirely escaped from it. He, who contends that salvation is intended for all, to the end of his days ascribes a peculiar claim to the Jew ; for his feeling is that of a Jewish patriot.[1] This patriotism begets in him the idea of a general conversion of Israel,[2] which, as the expression of such a feeling, is humanly comprehensible, but nevertheless very fantastic. It is, however, no falling off from his doctrine ; for he expects that Judaism will one day cease to be Jewish.

* * * * * * * *

3—The Origin of the Doctrine

Athene sprang armed in full power from the head of Zeus. The theology of Paul had no such origin. It grew and became, and we really understand it, like all other historical things, only so far as we can penetrate into its origin. No more than a very partial success can be attained in this attempt. Still, valuable perceptions may be gained, such as are likely to add more life to the

[1] Rom. 9¹⁻⁵.   [2] Rom. 11.

picture of that mass of thought which comes before us only in its finished state.

* * * * * * * *

A—The Heritage from Judaism

Paul had a theology already when he became a Christian. He was naturally unable to fling it away like a worn out cloak. The new way of regarding things which his conversion brought might indeed recast the old, but must necessarily take up a good part of it into itself. A new religion only engenders new ideas when, and so far as, it presents new religious realities. In faith in Jesus there were two, and only two new realities : *Jesus* himself, with his life, and the *community*. These shaped the original Christian thoughts, and are certainly the decisive realities ; but, being so few, they disappear before the Jewish ideas which merge into them or grow up unchanged by their side.

It can be definitely shown that a great Jewish heritage remains in the Pauline thought-world. It is indeed by no means unintelligible that Paul de Lagarde actually called this opponent of Judaism the most Jewish of all the apostles. As an educated theologian he possessed an especial wealth of clearly stamped Jewish ideas. Without too great trouble a tolerably comprehensive Jewish theology could be put together out of his letters ; the Jewish parallels would be easy to supply. We content ourselves with sketching a few leading elements.

About monotheism we need not speak. But the whole conception of the sway of the one God, how he lays his hand on history, accomplishes his purposes in it, foresees and foreordains, was not thought out for the first time by Paul the Christian. Those hard thoughts of God's predestination and almighty arbitrary will—he is gracious to whom he will, and whom he will he hardens[1]—had not indeed, in his pharisaic days, been applied to Israel, but were nevertheless not strange to him. Who could derive them from the idea of Christ, his death and his resurrection ? And everything that cannot be so derived is entirely Jewish.

The framework of the whole Pauline teaching is formed by the Jewish idea of a contrast between

---

[1] Rom. 9[18] sqq. [13].

two worlds (æons), one of which is present and
earthly, the other future and heavenly. Here
we have the foundation of the Pauline way of
regarding history. Here too is the Pauline
conception of salvation and bliss. The doctrine
that salvation is unattainable in this world,
because in its very nature it is a negation of
earth; that it is 'life,' permanency, glory—
betokens no change in the Jewish idea. To these
must be added the whole wealth of thoughts
about the future. All is Jewish, from the judgment with its wrath and retribution to the great
'oppression' before the end, to the 'blast of
the last trumpet,' to the victory of Messiah over
the hostile spirits.[1] Christ alone stands in a
new way in the centre of the picture; and yet
in the old way too, for the Jewish Messiah had
also his own place in the representation of the
future.

Another group of thoughts is concerned with
man. Paul's ethical pessimism is rooted in
Judaism. The universality of sin and the 'evil
heart' of man are known to the Jewish apocalyptic

[1] I Cor. 7²⁶, 15⁵², ²⁴ sqq.

books—even if they make some few exceptions.
They know too the devastating effects of the sin
of Adam. From him the ' abiding weakness '
in mankind derives its origin ; his fall is the fall
of all men.[1] In this way even the thought of
Christ as the representative of the new humanity
was half prefigured. What Jew would have found
anything new in the idea that death is the consequence and wages of sin ? It is a very irony
that all such specifically Jewish ideas are to-day
widely regarded as ' specifically Christian.'

The important effect, on Paul's doctrine, of
the Jewish belief in angels and demons has already
been touched on several times. The idea, again,
that the angels took part in the giving of the Law
on Sinai existed long before Paul. He was only
the first to use it—a sign of the extent to which
he lived in these conceptions—as a proof of the
worthlessness of the Law. But the conceptions
already mentioned by no means exhaust this
field. That the faithful shall one day judge the
angels, that women who do not cover their heads
during worship expose themselves to the lascivious

[1] For these thoughts cf. the so-called IV Ezra (3^{20} sqq.,
7^{118}) and the Apocalypse of Baruch.

gaze of the angels, that the stars, the heavenly bodies, are bodies of angelic beings[1]—not a few such thoughts, which are also taken over from Judaism, could be named.

It is not necessary to remind the reader again of the scripture, with its promise and its oracular predictions, of the significance which the Jewish view of the biblical history had for Paul— Abraham was celebrated as the hero of faith before Paul's time—of the estimate of heathendom and its cultus. Even then we should not exhaust the subject.[2] But this brief epitome is enough to show how important this world of Jewish thought was in its effect on Paul's comprehension of history. Nevertheless the chief question still is how the peculiarly Christian thoughts arose, which seized and leavened this Jewish material.

* * * * * * * *

B—The Origin of the 'Christian' Ideas

No doubt Paul's experience had a share in the formation of his doctrine. In his conversion he

---

[1] I Cor. 6³, 11¹⁰, 15⁴⁰ sq.

[2] Besides the purely Jewish ideas, Greek-Jewish (Hellenistic) ideas came into play.

experienced grace, his estimate of the Law underwent a change, his legalism received a shock ;
and if his thought concentrated itself so strongly
upon the death of Christ, this was an after-effect
of the fact that this death had previously been
to him the great ' offence.' Nevertheless the concrete thoughts of the apostle can only in a small
degree be explained as simply the reflex of his
experiences. .

Acute investigators would endeavour to show
how Paul came, by the mere necessities of logical
thinking, to develop his chief doctrines out of
his experiences together with his Jewish preconceptions. But their assumptions would be of
too doubtful a character for their conclusions
to be truly convincing. We know too little about
Paul's state at the time of his conversion and
about the thrust of his thought to say for certain
what inferences he *must* have formed. We must
here be content to work within limits.

According to the view which is really popular,
Paul, before the day of Damascus, was continually
and vainly wrestling for righteousness before God.
Instead of moral progress he suffered defeat after
defeat, and ever increasing despair. In such a

condition he beheld the apparition. This, therefore, brought him at once to perceive that only
grace, and never human conduct, could lead to
salvation. In this way the doctrine of justification
was the immediate fruit of it.

This view presupposes that this doctrine is
all in all to Paul. We have already seen that
this is a mistake (p. 123). But what have we to
say about this representation of the state of his
own soul ? Paul never speaks directly about this ;
but in that impressive picture of the fight of the
' inner man,' who desires the good, against the
stronger ' outer man ' and against sin, he is
supposed to have depicted his own experience.[1]
When, however, he uses the word ' I ' in this
passage we cannot take it as necessarily betokening
a real personal confession. In statements which
are of general validity I can speak in the first
person, and if they were all changed into the
second person, that would make no difference.
There are really good grounds for this interpretation : the ' I ' is always the unredeemed man ;
his misery is painted, and its gloom is so especially

[1] Rom. 7⁷⁻²⁵.

emphasized for the very reason that Paul is speaking from the standpoint of redemption.[1]

It must undoubtedly be admitted that the attitude of the Jew towards his Law had changed in the process of time. The old ingenuous confidence of ability to keep the Law, the joy of the Psalmist, which sang, ' I have delight in thy Law,' had largely yielded to a mood which felt the Law as an oppression and a burden. It is quite possible that Paul underwent depressing experiences of this kind in his striving after salvation, and to this extent his picture may include an element of personal experience. But that does not prove in the least that just before his conversion his soul was full of this one feeling. His own assertion that as a Pharisee he had lived irreproachably in the Law does not support this notion—the less, as his conversion was before his eyes as he wrote.[2]

---

[1] The passage certainly deals with a type. The continuation, 8[1], speaks quite generally of those that are in Christ. In 8[2] there appears, according to the common reading, an actual ' thou ' instead of the ' I.' 7[9] hardly admits of being taken as a description of experience, but expresses the dogmatic thesis that death is the punishment of sin.—Other grounds might be adduced, such as Jewish parallels.

[2] Phil. 3[6].

The truth is, the soul-strivings of Luther have stood as model for the portrait of Paul.[1]

And so disappears every inducement to derive the doctrine of justification and the rejection of the works of the Law directly from the conversion. To experience grace is not by any means the same thing as to set it up in contrast to human conduct. Belief in the death and resurrection of Christ is far from implying the necessity of doing away with circumcision and other rites, especially as Christ, in Paul's belief, had himself kept the Law.[2]

As we have already intimated (pp. 124 sq.), this doctrine had its immediate origin in the exigencies of Paul's mission to the Gentiles. It furnished the theoretical support for emancipation from Jewish institutions. In this case theory was the child, not the parent, of practice, even though the practice itself presupposes a depreciation of the institutions in question. Where Paul sets faith up in direct antithesis to these institutions he is dealing with the practical question, what

[1] It must not be forgotten that Paul does not treat the question of 'works' as a personal question; he has Judaism and its principle always in mind.

[2] Gal. 4[4]; Rom. 15[8].

makes a man a Christian. His rejection of the
whole Law, as the embodiment of the principle
of works, was no doubt a later development.

* * * * * * * *

A far more important question is, what was
the origin of the Pauline conception of Christ ?[1]
For those, indeed, who see in Jesus what Paul
saw, a supramundane, divine being, no problem
arises. But those who take Jesus for what he
was, an historical human personality, perceive an
enormous gulf between this man and the Pauline
Son of God. Not a generation had passed away
since the death of Jesus, and already his form had
not only grown into the infinite, but been utterly
changed. How came that to pass ?

*The picture of Christ did not originate in an
impression of the personality of Jesus.* This view
has often been maintained, but never adequately
supported with proof.

Paul in all probability never saw Jesus ; certainly never received any personal impression of
him ; if he had received such an impression it must
necessarily have been of such a kind as allowed
him to become Jesus' persecutor. How much he

[1] This exposition is supplemented in Chapter IV.

had learnt from the adherents of Jesus about his life and person, before he reached his conception of Christ, is difficult to say. He himself denies that he received any instruction from the original apostles in the time after his conversion.[1] But if, in the face of probability, we assume that he had at an early date heard much about Jesus, it only becomes the more astonishing that this possessed no significance for his mind. We already know that what was most important to him in the humanity of Jesus was not the ethical and religious value of his person or his earthly life, but his abnegation of his divine existence. In the actual ' life ' of Jesus—we exclude the assumption of humanity and the resurrection—only one event is important to Paul, namely the destruction of that life, Jesus' death. But again this is not, in his eyes, the moral act of a man—he is as far as possible from martyr-worship in this sense—it is indeed no historical fact at all; it transcends history; it is an occurrence in a world above that of sense. For, without its redeeming power, it is nothing.

The human personality of Jesus could be regarded as determinative in one case, and in

[1] Gal. 1¹⁶ sq.; cf. ¹².

one case alone : if the Christology appeared as an idealization, transformation, apotheosis of Jesus, so that the historical reality could still shine through it. But this is certainly not the case with Paul. Or could the humility, obedience, and love which fill the Son of God when he exchanges heaven for the misery of earth be a reflexion of Jesus, the meek and merciful man ? Could Paul have gathered the manifold features of the character of Jesus into a magnificent synthesis, and translated them into the celestial mode ? It has been so supposed, but wrongly. Christ is called obedient because he did not oppose the divine decision to send him for the salvation of the world, although it cost him his divine nature, and brought him to the cross ; he is called meek, because he humbled himself to the lowliness of earth. Love must have been his motive, because his incarnation and his death were of the highest possible benefit to man. Such a benefit springs naturally from the desire to benefit, that is from love.[1] None of these ethical

---

[1] For this reason, too, the idea of the love of Christ is constantly interchanging with that of the love of God : e.g. Rom. 5⁸.

predicates, therefore, is taken from an impression of the moral character of Jesus ; all originate in the apostle's own doctrine of redemption.

This account is, however, still imperfect. The chief question is, can it be considered possible that Paul himself exalted Jesus into the heavenly Son of God ? This consideration does not affect only the attempt to derive the Pauline Christ-ology from an impression of Jesus' personality. It affects with equal force the opinion that the apostle drew—either from the celestial existence of the risen Jesus, or from other thoughts—the ' conclusion ' that the Christ must have existed before his earthly life. The other view that a sort of ' impulse ' to ' exalt ' the dignity of Jesus led Paul to make, out of the human Messiah of the original community, the superhuman Son of God, is equally untenable. According to all these views the germ of this Christology would be a product of Paul's mind, a work of his imagina-tion ; and that is an impossibility. The magnifi-cent assurance, confidence, and enthusiasm of his faith would be utterly unintelligible, if its foundation were a conception which he had him-self excogitated.

There remains only one explanation : *Paul believed in such a celestial being, in a divine Christ, before he believed in Jesus.* Until he became a Christian it seemed to him sacrilege to call Jesus the Christ. This man did not answer at all to the divine figure of Christ which Paul bore within him. But in the moment of conversion, when Jesus appeared before him in the shining glory of his risen existence, Paul identified him with his own Christ, and straightway transferred to Jesus all the conceptions which he already had of the celestial being—for instance, that he had existed before the world and had taken part in its creation. The man Jesus was really, therefore, only the wearer of all those mighty predicates which had already been established ; but the bliss of the apostle lay in this, that he could now regard what had hitherto been a mere hope, as a tangible reality which had come into the world. Here again we see the great importance of the fact that he had not known Jesus. Intimate disciples could not so readily believe that the man with whom they had sat at table in Capernaum, or sailed on the Lake of Galilee, was the creator of the world. But in Paul's way there was no such obstacle.

If Paul was acquainted with this divine Christ before his conversion, there must have been circles in Judaism which held the same belief. But can such a belief in this field be really authenticated ? So much is certain, that Jewish apocalyptic books are really cognizant of a Messiah, who before his appearance lives in heaven, and is more exalted than the angels themselves. This is a datum of the highest importance. Whether, however, every feature in the Pauline Christ can be explained by means of the extant apocalyptic accounts of Messiah, is a question we shall not here attempt to decide. Investigation is only now beginning to master the problem aright. The immediate point of supreme importance is the perception of this fact : that the Pauline Christ cannot be understood unless we assume that Paul, while still a Pharisee, possessed a number of definite conceptions concerning a divine being, which were afterwards transferred to the historical Jesus.[1]

[1] Such assumptions are not necessary in Paul's case alone. In John, for instance, when Jesus is called ' the Word ' (the Logos), this is the appropriation to Jesus of a religious conception which was already in circulation.

Still, Paul's view of Christ was affected by the conversion to this extent, that the human life of Jesus, with its culmination in death and resurrection, became a part of the picture. In the whole life of the celestial being this human existence formed no more than a transitory phase, but nevertheless the death and resurrection were, for mankind, nothing else than the redemption.

The following, then, may serve as an epitome of the whole development.

First comes the idea of Christ. On this the whole conception of the redemption rests. For the death and resurrection of Christ are not regarded as the experiences of a man, but as the experiences of an incarnate *divine* being. It is upon this that their universal, world-redeemed significance depends. The key to the problem, in itself so enigmatical, why the Son of God became a man, was found by Paul in this twofold event. The idea of the redemption itself was again determined by the conceptions which the apostle brought with him. He expected his Christ to vanquish the evil powers of the world, including the demons, and to inaugurate a new condition of things. The accomplishment of this task was found, where but in the two events of salvation ? How Paul came to find it there must remain an open question. Probably these thoughts had long been definitely formulated in his mind before he was led by polemical exigencies to mint the doctrine of justification.

PAUL'S PLACE IN THE HISTORY OF CHRISTIAN ORIGINS

1—Paul and the Previous Development (Jesus; the Original Community)

THE importance of Paul's religious position can only be clearly apprehended if we compare him with the original community, and chiefly with Jesus himself. Such a comparison may well appear precarious, while the degree and the form in which the thoughts of Jesus have been handed down to us are so insecure. But the decisive points lie clearly before our eyes. It must, however, be generally borne in mind that only the earliest stratum of the material of our first three gospels existed before the elaboration of the Pauline theology; a great part of it came into being alongside or after that theology, and even— here and there—under its influence.

Jesus and Paul do not belong to the same
stratum of Judaism. The wisdom of the rabbis,
the visionary speculation of the apocalyptic
writers, the atmosphere of Hellenistic thought
were to Paul what the plain piety of simple people
was to Jesus. The whole religious language of
Paul is on another level from the language of
Jesus. It moves in a wealth of concepts, which
are treated and employed as concepts. The
phenomena of the religious life are ranged under
general categories, such as 'Sin.' Reflection is
always at work ; religion is not to be severed from
thinking and thoughts. Jesus, on the other
hand, has a simple, almost elementary language ;
few, but mightily effective religious ideas. Here
is no important collaboration of the intellect, no
juxtaposition and distinction of concepts, no
complicated series of thoughts ; but only a perfectly clear application of established and fundamental religious ideas to the practice of the religious
life, with especial regard to the conscience and
the will.

It might therefore be supposed that Paul, with
the help of his circle of concepts, applied to the
'gospel of Jesus' a theological mode of apprehen-

sion, gave it a theological mintage and mould, was in fact the *theological expounder and successor of Jesus.*

This is indeed the prevalent view in modern theology. Julius Wellhausen, the pioneer in Old Testament criticism, has even affirmed with emphasis that Paul was truly the man who understood the gospel of Jesus. Adolf Harnack and many others have repeated it. Nevertheless, I am unable to concur in this judgment ; I rather see in it no slight historical error.

* * * * * * * *

What is the real extent of the influence which the preaching of Jesus—of course only through the agency of the immediate disciples or the original community—exercised on Paul ?

Many lines of connexion may unquestionably be drawn from the one to the other ; but these by no means suffice to demonstrate an influence of Jesus on Paul. Both men belong to the Judaism of the same age. It is then self-evident that their religion must of necessity exhibit a number of features in common. Must we, for instance, look to the preaching of Jesus for an explanation, if Paul calls God ' our father,' or

glories in being a child of God ? Long before
Jesus Judaism was acquainted with the divine
name ' father,' and thought of God not only as
the father of Israel, but of each individual man ;
it is not even true that Jesus was the first to
set this name in the forefront.[1]   In the same way
Judaism counted childhood or sonship of God
among the essential benefits of religion.   But that
special *aspect* of God which Jesus associates with
the name of father—he directs and governs all,
cares with inexhaustible kindness for each, counts
the very hairs of our head—this, with the special
note of trust in God which corresponds to it,
scarcely finds an echo in Paul.—It is equally
doubtful, in spite of considerable correspondences,
whether the Pauline picture of the future can be
considered a propagation of original thoughts of
Jesus.

Assuredly many precepts and rules of Jesus
were traditionally known to Paul, and he assuredly
regarded them as of standard authority.[2]   It is
quite possible that in such exhortations as ' bless

[1] This is convincingly shown by the Wisdom of Solomon,
2[16-18], where it is actually put forward as the sign of a pious
man that he calls God his father.

[2] I Cor. 7[10], 9[14] (cf. 11[23] sqq.).

your persecutors '[1] we have an echo of current
sayings of Jesus ; but it is not certain, for Judaism
was also acquainted with such thoughts. To
love our neighbour was probably to Paul, as to all
Christians, an established ' commandment of the
Lord.' But it did not mean to him what it meant
to Jesus, and is in reality eclipsed by love of
associates in church and faith, by ' love of the
brethren ' ; and this virtue in a community may
have been emphasized in the Jewish Dispersion
more than we know. Whether, however, the
points of material contact with Jesus in this
field be more or less numerous, the special moral
atmosphere of the sayings of Jesus, their powerful,
majestic style, their critical keenness, their stress
upon truth of heart, have never, one may say,
been felt by any finely sensitive soul in the moral
preaching of Paul.

It appears very obvious that Paul's aversion
from the Jewish institutions and his liberation
of the gospel from all national barriers is a consistent carrying out of the attitude of Jesus.
But at this precise point the independence of

[1] Rom. 12[14]

Paul is easy to recognize. Moreover, he does not appeal in his polemic even once to Jesus' posture of freedom towards the Law. And this is no mere accident, as is proved by something else : it is part of his faith that Jesus lived in strict accordance with the Law, and he accounts this a part of the humiliation of the Son of God : Christ passed under the Law, and became a servant of the circumcision.[1]

Paul's motives, too, at this point, are manifestly quite other than those of Jesus.[2] Jesus' attack on the character of the Law is always of a moral kind. He assails the institutions when and because they slay the moral sense, rob the soul of piety, substitute appearance for reality. Where in Paul's work do we find such an ethical criticism of legalism ? He fights against the Law as a missionary, and as the advocate of redemption in Christ. That is another matter. Once more, Jesus, by seeing and desiring to see in the Jew only the man, depreciates the national privileges :

[1] Gal. 4⁴ ; Rom. 15⁸.

[2] Consistently with this, the two are concerned to a great extent with quite different sides of the Law. Circumcision— a chief point with Paul—could never have been to Jesus an object of polemic.

Paul proclaims salvation for all mankind : is that the same ? A certain affinity may be perceived, but the real sense is essentially different; [1] the reason why Paul declared all national distinctions to be indifferent was not that he had ' understood Jesus.'

* * * * * * * *

The question what influence Jesus' preaching had on Paul hardly brings many really important facts to light. But it is not after all the decisive question. The main question is, what was *the real distance between the Pauline doctrine and the preaching of Jesus ?* A comparison of details would here be futile ; we must keep in view the central point on each side.

Jesus says, ' Be ye perfect, as your heavenly father is perfect.' Paul says, ' He who did not spare his own son, how should he not give us all things together with him ? '

Jesus says, ' If thine eye offend [tempt] thee, cast it away ; it is better for thee to enter with

---

[1] Only in one passage, Rom. 2^{17-29}, can we trace a close affinity with the spirit of the sayings of Jesus ; and this passage is of subordinate importance in the Pauline exposition as a whole.

M

one eye into the kingdom of God than to be cast
with two eyes into hell.' Paul says, ' Christ is
become unto us the wisdom of God, unto righteousness, salvation, and redemption.'

Jesus says, ' No man can serve two masters ;
. . . . . ye cannot serve God and mammon.'
Paul says, ' Christ was yielded up for our sins
and raised again for our justification.'

Jesus says, ' No man who has laid his hand on
the plough and looks back is fit for the kingdom
of God.' Paul says, ' God has rescued us from the
power of darkness and transferred us into the
kingdom of the Son of his love.'[1]

These may be affirmed to be utterances in which,
on both sides, the character of the whole comes
into view.

In Jesus everything aims at the personal
character of the individual. Man shall yield his
soul whole and undivided to God and God's will.
Most of Jesus' preaching has, for this reason, the
imperative form, or at least an imperative character. True, the moral appeal is everywhere
backed by reward and punishment, and these are

[1] Jesus : Matt. 5⁴⁸ ; Mark 9⁴⁷ ; Matt. 6²⁴ ; Luke 9⁶².
Paul : Rom. 8³² ; I Cor. 1³⁰ ; Rom. 4²⁵ ; Col. 1¹³.

to Jesus by no means superfluous ideas ; but their chief end is to make men feel the stern earnestness of the will of God, and the greatness of human responsibility. The preaching of Jesus certainly exhibits other features, but its heart is to be found, if anywhere, in these things.

In Paul the central point is a divine act, in history but transcending history, or a complex of such acts, which impart to all mankind a ready-made salvation. Whoever believes in these divine acts—the incarnation, death, and resurrection of a celestial being, receives salvation.

And this, which to Paul is the sum of religion— the skeleton of the fabric of his piety, without which it would collapse—can this be a continuation or a remoulding of the gospel of Jesus ? Where, in all this, is that gospel to be found, which Paul is said to have understood ?

Of that which is to Paul all and everything, how much does Jesus know ? Nothing whatever. Let people point as often as they will to his claim to have been chosen as Messiah ; it must still be doubted—in spite of a few places in the gospels which assert as much—that he ever made himself an object of faith or doctrine. It is as improbable as anything could be that he ever assigned to his death a saving power, although this thought also has once or twice made its way into the gospels.[1]

On the other hand, Paul certainly shows a series of points of contact with the sayings of Jesus. But everything of that kind belongs, in Paul, to the second rank of importance. The *kernel* of his gospel lies elsewhere.

Let us consider, too, not only 'views,' but devoutness itself, as something subjective. Great as is Paul's ethical interest, there is no doubt that he subordinated the moral virtues of character to something else, and not only in polemic ; to faith or belief, that is, to a conviction with a quite definite, formulable content, at bottom belief in a dogma—however it may be distinguished, and however much to the advantage of its simplicity and cordiality, from the cold and laborious definitions of later times. We may put it : in Paul's mind the first question is whether a man is a member of the church. No human excellence can confer any worth upon him so

---

[1] Mark 10⁴⁵, 14²⁴.

long as he does not fulfil this condition, so long as
he does not believe in the crucified and risen
Son of God. This faith recognizes, indeed, no
barriers of race, but it becomes itself a barrier,
which separates two classes of men. Purely
human standards of morality to judge piety
withal, such as Jesus used, are on this account
excluded from Paul's world.

To reproach Paul is idle. He did not put a
religion together by mere caprice, but was guided
by internal and external necessity. But the facts
themselves must not be whittled down. And, if
we do not wish to deprive both figures of all
historical distinctness, the name 'disciple of
Jesus' has little applicability to Paul, if it is
used to denote an historical relation. In comparison with Jesus Paul is essentially a new
phenomenon, as new, considering the large basis
of common ground, as he could possibly be. He
stands much farther away from Jesus than Jesus
himself stands from the noblest figures of Jewish
piety. It does not help us to say that Paul cannot
teach like Jesus, *because* he looks back upon
the figure and the life of Jesus. We need not
repeat that the life-work and life-picture of Jesus

did *not* determine the Pauline theology. This fact cannot be shaken—let Paul have known as much about Jesus as he will, let him have been moved by accounts of him more deeply than we know, let him even on occasion in his missionary preaching have reported this or that about Jesus. He, indeed, felt himself to be a disciple and apostle of Jesus, and felt it his honour to be so ; he was not conscious of his innovations. But in view of the facts this is really far enough from proving that he was only a continuator of Jesus' work. and that he understood Jesus ; and, besides, the being whose disciple and apostle he wished to be was not actually the historical man Jesus, but another.

We see then that in the very first decades of nascent Christianity a great leap forward was made in the development of the religion itself. At first sight extremely perplexing, this becomes on a nearer view intelligible. Paul had had no contact with Jesus himself, and was therefore much further removed from him than his nearness in point of time would indicate. His faith had been attained through a ' revelation,' and in consequence he was able to apprehend and interpret the vision of Jesus by means of ideas of Christ whose origin was quite independent of Jesus the man.

Another thing must be remembered. Between Jesus and Paul stands the original community. It is the precondition of Paul's existence, and forms beyond doubt a kind of bridge from the one to the other. In consequence of the visions of Christ, the most important matter even for the Jerusalem community was an 'event of salvation': Jesus is risen. Even for them the distinguishing mark which parted them from Judaism was an utterance of faith: Jesus is proven the Messiah, and will as Messiah appear in glory. Even they considered the death of Jesus a fulfilment of prophecy, and therefore a 'Messianic' event. Without considerable elements of identity between the faith of Paul and that of the real disciples of Jesus their whole relation to one another, and their consciousness of a really existent religious communion, would be inconceivable. And yet the divergence between the mother church and Paul is very great, and in truth greater than the parties themselves knew. Once for all the whole horizon is altered: it is no more the Jewish nation that forms the frame for

all ideas, but the world, humanity. Christ is
no more the Jewish Messiah, but the saviour
of the world ; faith in him is therefore no more
a form of the Jewish faith, but a new faith.
And secondly the Christology is new; not merely
because the man Jesus meant much more to
the mother community than to Paul, but chiefly
because in Paul the origin and nature of Christ
has become celestial. Out of this grows, in the
third place, an essentially new estimate of the
death of Christ. We must leave it here un-
decided whether the original Christian society
had already come to look upon it as a death
' for sin ' ;[1] even then it would have been to
them only an isolated occurrence, which they
were glad to be able, not merely to justify,
but also positively to prize. Whereas in Paul
the death of Jesus (with the resurrection) has
become absolutely the peculiar mystery of the
redemption of the world, the foundation of all.
That Paul's treatment of history is as a whole

[1] The cogent evidence for this view is generally seen in
I Cor. 15³. But it requires a very literal interpretation of
Paul's words to make out that what was delivered to him
includes ' died *for our sins*.'

something essentially new, follows of itself from what has been said.

* * * * * * * *

2—Paul's Influence upon his Age

We shall not enquire how great an esteem Paul commanded after his death in the Gentile church of which he was the pioneer ; let it suffice if we point to such influence of his thoughts as can be traced upon the succeeding age.

The natural media for the continuance of his spiritual force were first, in an especial sense, his trusted disciples and helpers. But what they really accomplished in this capacity is altogether obscure. This brings out all the clearer a new kind of influence which the apostle began to exercise some time after his death. His letters were not, in their origin, literary productions ; they were purely personal utterances, intended for small circles, with all the particular characteristics of real letters. But now that they were collected and circulated they gained in greater and greater degree a public acceptance, an authoritative significance for the whole church ; in the end they became canonical. In this way, after his death and without his co-operation, Paul became a literary entity. His influence in this character is to a great extent confused by us with the movement of which he was the active centre in his lifetime.

The traces of his effective influence are palpable enough in the epistolary literature which sprung up after him. His style was imitated, the forms of his letters were copied, letters were published under his name. But this fact has, after all, no very great historical importance. A desire to do honour to Paul, or to count as his adherent, is no true measure of real spiritual communion with him. For instance, the letters to Timothy and Titus, though they employ many Pauline turns of speech, are remote indeed, in their whole character, from Paul. And if certain writings, especially the epistle to the Ephesians and the first epistle of Peter, evince a real understanding of his thoughts, that is still only a subordinate matter. The real operative influence of the apostle cannot be apprehended by considering such special literary results. Unless it appears in the whole breadth of the later development of faith and doctrine it does not count for much.

As a whole, as a structure with a character of its own, we must admit that the Pauline theology can never again be found in later times. And that is natural enough, if only because it always remained the theology of a born Jew, and even a Pharisee ; because, in other words, it rested upon a number of preconceptions which later Christians neither possessed nor could artificially adopt.

And yet, without exaggeration, we can assign to it a mighty after-effect. We see this especially when we think of the conception of Christ and his work. The nature of subjective piety is often far aloof from Paul ; but the utterances about Christ as a celestial being who assumed flesh, about the ' saviour of the world ' who descended to earth, meet us everywhere, and so do the thoughts of the redemptive power of his death, even though the formulas often deviate somewhat from Paul.

Nothing can throw so much light on the whole matter as the Johannine gospel, which has itself had so mighty an effect. This writing cannot, indeed, be entirely explained, in the peculiar stamp of its own thoughts, by means of Paul : but Paul is beyond all doubt its foundation. When the

Johannine Christ recounts how he was with the
Father before he became flesh, it is Paul himself
who is speaking to us; and when in this gospel
John the Baptist extols Jesus as the Lamb of
God, that takes away the sins of the world, the
voice again is that of Paul. It is true that since
Paul the view of the life of Jesus has been fundamentally altered. The Messianic glory of Jesus
was originally looked for in the future, not in his
life on earth. Gradually but continuously this
earthly life has taken a stronger Messianic colour.
Jesus was not only the Messiah that should come,
but the Messiah that had come. As early as John
the whole life on earth is nothing but a continual
radiance of divine glory. But precisely for this
reason Paul's ideas were able to find expression
in this very story. The Pauline Son of God
could now be shown in the flesh. In fact, the
Pauline doctrine of Christ was, in John, poured
into the mould of an image of the earthly life,
and in this way won a new charm and new power
over our hearts.

The fate of the Pauline doctrine of justification
has often excited astonishment. Echoes of it
are to be found, but it can clearly be seen that

these are only formulas which have been conservatively retained, and are but half understood. The dominating view, everywhere quite frankly expressed, is that the way to salvation is to keep the commandments of God, and of course also the commandment to believe.

In reality it is not so strange that that doctrine practically disappears, especially if it was, as we found, a polemical doctrine. It disappears because the situation for which it was devised has disappeared. The question which at one time exercised every mind, how the converted heathen must stand towards the Jewish Law, lost in the course of things all practical importance. It became self-evident that the Law could not assert any claim. What need was there, then, of the theory ? But the doctrine that the works of men have no importance at all for salvation was perhaps never very widely understood, and was often instinctively rejected by the moral sense. The Jewish ideas with which Paul was dealing were naturally even more alien to the later mind.

In spite of all, however, this polemical doctrine has left a very beneficial result behind it. It has in fact had the effect of making itself superfluous, and that is no small matter. With the exception of insignificant groups the whole church since Paul rejects the Jewish particularism ; the saying that in Christ there is neither Jew nor Greek has become a common possession. And to this a second fact may be added : the whole church rejects, consciously and completely, the Jewish ceremonial Law, and feels that her freedom from the Law distinguishes her essentially from the Jewish religion. In general, moreover, she feels herself completely sundered from that religion, much more than Paul himself did ; a generation after Paul the last link with Judaism had been severed.

The immediate importance of these things in the inner life of piety has been but little. In the development of the church they have been fundamental.

On various sides, then, the spiritual stamp of the church of that age was decisively determined by Paul. But it is not enough to consider him in the frame of his own time. His figure has exercised a continuous influence throughout the centuries of history of the Christian church and culture.   *   *   *   *   *   *   *   *

Paul's Importance in the History of the World

What Paul has been for the Christian religion can be comprised in three sentences :—

1. By his missionary labour he transplanted it to a new soil, the actual world of Græco-Roman culture.

2. He not only lifted the Christian religion out of the narrowness of Judaism, but tore it loose from Judaism itself, and gave the Christian community for the first time the consciousness of being a new religion.

3. He was the first Christian theologian, and by means of his theology he decisively transformed the incipient religion.

Let us consider these three points somewhat more exactly.

Firstly. The missionary ministry of Paul mightily enhanced the impulse to the dissemination of Christianity, and laid the first foundation in the new faith of the sense of strength, the consciousness of a power and a duty to conquer. And yet this is not the most important thing.

When Paul came on the scene the faith in Jesus dwelt in a corner of the world ; it led its quiet life on Semitic soil. When Paul died it had settled in numerous places in the real world of culture, and its centre of gravity had already been removed from Semitic ground. This geographical transference was of enormous importance for the unfolding of the new religion, and meant the opening of a way for its most eventful intrinsic development. By entering into the domain of heathendom the Christian religion necessarily undergoes transformation, assimilates much of the religion and thought of Gentile peoples, is constrained to revise both its apologetic and its propaganda, and so to develop new ideas and ways of life.

Secondly. It was not in Paul's original intention to set Christianity free from Judaism ; it was the evolution of the work of his life which of itself forced him to such a step. This act of his appears all the greater, since he himself remains, to a certain extent, under the sway of his Jewish past. The practical man and the thinker, however, here join hands. What really accomplishes the rejection of Jewish rules of life is the idea, conceived and established by Paul, of the independence and newness of the Christian religion. Before him there was only a Jewish sect, which had gathered about Jesus; when he died there existed a Christian church, which intended to be the salt of the whole earth.

Thirdly. Movements in a theological direction were not unknown to the original community; the recognition of the Old Testament was enough to beget them. But Paul is still the real creator of a Christian theology.

The step from religion to theology is always of fundamental importance. It is felt at first to be a descent, from what is simple, immediate, natural to something complicated, secondary, reflected. But it is also felt to be a necessity, a set condition for the maintenance and progress of religion, and so far a gain. The significance of a religion for the world of culture depends on its assigning a part to the intellect, that is to say, on its generating a theology.

Even more important is the question what it was that Paul the theologian effected; *how* he remoulded the new religion. The least part of it is his introduction of a considerable rabbinical element into Christianity. Everything, on the other hand, is said when we say he made Christianity the religion of redemption. True, we may

N

say of all real religion that it is and intends to be redemptive, but it is not of this general truth that we are thinking when we characterize particular religions as religions of redemption.

No one who set out to describe the religion which lives in the sayings and similitudes of Jesus could hit by any chance on the phrase ' religion of redemption.' The idea of redemption glimmers, it is true, in the future hope, the kingdom of God : but it does not belong to the essence of the matter. The emphasis falls on individual piety, and its connexion with future salvation. But in Paul, on the other hand, religion *is* nothing else but an appropriated and experienced redemption.

That which redeems, however, is by no means to be found in man himself, but outside of him in a divine work of redemption, which has prepared salvation for mankind once for all. In other words it lies in the history which has been transacted between God and man, in the ' history of salvation ' or the ' acts of salvation.' Paul's whole innovation is comprised in this, that *he laid the foundation of religion in these acts of salvation, in the incarnation, death, and resurrection of Christ.*

If we are to designate the character of this conception we cannot avoid the word 'myth.' We do not employ it with the desire to hurt anyone's feelings. It is not, as we use it, an expression of contempt. A doctrine whose profundity has endowed millions of hearts with the best of their possessions, a doctrine without which such men as Luther, Paul Gerhard, and Johann Sebastian Bach could not have been, a doctrine which even to-day comforts and fills with peace thousands upon thousands of good and earnest people, a doctrine which has given the thoughts of divine love and grace and of human sinfulness their most powerful expression, such a doctrine we treat with reverence. But the nature of the thought that a divine being forsakes heaven, veils himself in humanity and then dies, in order to ascend again into heaven, is not altered by such considerations as these. To one who cannot give credence to it it is necessarily, in its own essence, a mythological conception.

It follows then conclusively from all this that Paul is to be regarded as *the second founder of Christianity*. As a rule even liberal theology shrinks from this conclusion. But it is not to be

evaded. For Paul it demonstrably was who first
—even if a certain preparative work had already
been done—introduced into Christianity the ideas
whose influence in its history up to the present
time has been deepest and most wide-reaching.
Tertullian, Origen, Athanasius, Augustine, Anselm
of Canterbury, Luther, Calvin, Zinzendorf—not
one of these great teachers can be understood on
the ground of the preaching and historic personality of Jesus ; their Christianity cannot be
comprehended as a remodelling of ' the gospel ' ;
the key to their comprehension, though of course
sundry links stand between, is Paul. The back-
bone of Christianity for all of them was the history
of salvation ; they lived for that which they
shared with Paul. This second founder of Christianity has even, compared with the first, exercised
beyond all doubt the stronger—not the better—
influence. True, he has not lorded it everywhere,
especially not in the life of simple, practical piety,
but throughout long stretches of church history—
one need but think of the Councils and dogmatic
contests—he has thrust that greater person,
whom he meant only to serve, utterly into the
background.

But this reshaping of Christianity was manifestly a precondition for his work of setting it up, over against Judaism, as a religion with a principle of its own. Without his theology of redemption he would not have been able to treat Judaism as a superseded religion. He preserved the new faith from pining away as a Jewish sect ; he rescued it for history ; but he did this by transforming its character.

Paul is, in truth, a figure grand enough to have a place in the world's history. We need not think for a moment of those special incentives and suggestions which an Augustine or a Luther found in him. What enabled him to accomplish the task of his life was that religiously, as well as intellectually and morally, he was an extraordinary personality ; and no doubt this also, that he had not become a Christian in the normal way. The ' revelation ' freed him from the fetters of tradition in which the members of the mother community were bound ; it gave him the power to make a new beginning.

Jesus or Paul : this alternative characterizes, at least in part, the religious and theological warfare of the present day. The older school of

belief is no doubt convinced that with Paul it
enters, for the first time, into possession of the
whole and genuine Jesus; and it is also able,
to a certain extent, to take up the historical Jesus
into its Pauline Christ. Still, this Christ must
needs for the most part crush out the man Jesus.
On the other hand, even the 'modern theology'
is not willing to forsake Paul. Paul is rich
enough to afford them precious thoughts, such as
they can make entirely their own. It finds
especially congenial Paul's fight against the Law,
although the 'protestant' element in that contest
is readily over-estimated. But in Paul's own
mind all this, without the kernel of his Christology,
is nothing, and no honour paid to the great
personality can compensate for the surrender of
this kernel. As a whole Paul belongs absolutely
to ecclesiastical orthodoxy, whether it preserves his
views quite faithfully in matters of detail or not.

But the serious questions of many kinds which
are raised by our presentment of Paul must be
commended to the reader's own deliberation.
We could only set ourself the task of apprehend-
ing and estimating Paul from a purely historical
point of view.

APPENDIX

PAULINE LITERATURE

Works on PAUL for the general reader, in the strict sense, are :—

Wernle : Paul as Missionary to the Gentiles, 1899 (Lecture).

† Weinel : Paul, the Man and his Work : the Beginnings of Christianity, the Church, and Dogma, 1904.

Weinel : Paul as Organizer, 1899 (a small work).

Bousset : The Apostle Paul, 1898 (a short sketch).

Works also intended for a larger circle of readers, but of a more scientific character :—

Hausrath : The Apostle Paul, 2nd Ed., 1872 (a biography).

Clemen : Paul, his Life and Work, 1904—the second volume, complete in itself.

Besides these we name only such scientific works as do not require technical learning in the reader, or can be used by untechnical students who, though educated, have no command of the Greek language. The chief of these is Renan's Paul ; large sections too of the following works may be consulted :—

† Weizsäcker : The Apostolic Age, 2nd Ed.,1892. (On Paul's theology, mission, and work in founding communities.)

Pfleiderer : Early Christianity, its Writings and Doctrines, 2nd Ed., 1902, Vol. i. (Personality, letters, theology.)

† Wernle : The Beginnings of our Religion, 2nd Ed., 1904. (Especially theology.)

The innumerable, and in part highly important, mono-graphs and writings on special points must be excluded from this survey.

Of the works above named those marked thus (†) have appeared in English translations. The English reader may also consult the articles on Paul, Acts, and the several Epistles in Hastings' Dictionary of the Bible and the 'Encyclopædia Biblica.'